18988944

THE ENTREPRENEUR IN MICROECONOMIC THEORY

THE ENTREPRENEUR IN MICROECONOMIC THEORY

Disappearance and Explanation

Humberto Barreto

Routledge
London and New York

First published 1989 by Routledge
11 New Fetter Lane, London EC4P 4EE
29 West 35th Street, New York, NY 10001

© 1989 Humberto Barreto

Phototypeset by Input Typesetting Ltd. London
Printed and bound in Great Britain by
Biddles Ltd. Guildford and King's Lynn

British Library Cataloguing in Publication Data

Barreto, Humberto, *1960–*
    The entrepreneur in microeconomic theory:
    disappearance and explanation
    I. Title
    338.5

    ISBN 0–415–00929–4

Library of Congress Cataloging in Publication Data

Barreto, Humberto, 1960–
    The entrepreneur in microeconomic theory.
    Bibliography: p.
    Includes index.
    1. Entrepreneurship. 2. Microeconomics. I. Title.
HB615.B37   1989   338'.04   88–32546
ISBN 0–415–00929–4

To my best friend, Tami,
and my daughter, Tyler

Contents

List of tables

List of figures

Preface

I have found it quite difficult to put 'finishing touches' on this book and send it in for final publication. I know there are many other changes that could be made to improve the exposition and style, but I also know that this process would go on indefinitely if my goal were to write the perfect book. Thus, in a thinly veiled attempt to head off criticism, I offer the following excuses.

To the reader who thinks certain sections are too simplistic, I ask for your patience. The exposition must allow the non-expert access to modern microeconomic theory if the argument is to have any hope of being understood. I have assumed a basic working knowledge of the theory of the firm (including its constituent isoquant, output, and factor market optimization problems), but have tried to explain carefully how the pieces of the theory fit together.

To the reader who thinks certain sections are too technical or mathematical, I suggest you examine an intermediate microtheory textbook and graduate level microtheory text. Once again, it is important that the modern theory of the firm and the orthodox theory of value be well understood – especially the interrelations between various facets of the overall theory.

To the reader who thinks a full-scale diatribe against orthodox microeconomic theory is in order, I am sorry to disappoint you. Modern microtheory does many things well, not the least of which is to present a logically tight, internally consistent theoretical structure. Anyone who disagrees with this is bucking over a half-century of economic thought. The point of this book is not that microtheory cannot do anything right, but that its beneficial points come at a cost – the loss of the entrepreneur. This leaves the orthodox economist without an historically key player in the explanation of the market system. And thus economics must swing back and rediscover the entrepreneur, especially as technological change becomes increasingly important.

It is quite unfair, however, to say that the wrong decision was made in the 1930s or to replay Jevons' charge against Ricardo and argue that Hicks Samuelson *et al.* 'shunted the car of economic science on the wrong track'. At the time, the development of the theory of the firm was a significant accomplishment – the culmination of years of hard work – and had confused Leon Walras the man Schumpeter credits as the greatest pure theorist of all time. But time passes and economic theory must advance. It is here that the heretic will agree with my charge that the very property, consistency, which made the theory initially appealing is now preventing orthodox microeconomics from considering radically different approaches. This is a situation that can be remedied only by the emergence of completely different, totally incommensurable research programs. Obviously, time will tell.

Of course, all errors and omissions are my own, but I would like to thank those people who supported my efforts. Professor Vincent J. Tarascio spent many hours discussing the ideas contained herein and provided useful comments. Professor Israel Kirzner kindly agreed to read the manuscript and encouraged me to publish it. Scott Hemmerlein helped proof the manuscript and construct the tables and graphs. Finally, I wish to thank my friends at the University of North Carolina and Wabash College for listening to me bemoan the disappearance of the entrepreneur and complain about the failures of orthodox economics.

Introduction

The entrepreneur has played a wide variety of functional roles throughout the history of economic thought. From Richard Cantillon, writing before Adam Smith, to the present-day Austrian economics revival, the entrepreneur has been cast as a fundamental agent in production, distribution, and growth theories. The entrepreneur has been a coordinator, arbitrageur, innovator, and uncertainty-bearer in theories spanning place, time, and problem orientation.

Since the 1930s, however, orthodox microeconomic theory has removed entrepreneurial considerations from its explanatory structure; the entrepreneur 'virtually disappeared from the theoretical literature'.[1] The word 'entrepreneur' may still occasionally be used, but it has lost any real meaning. Entrepreneurship, in any of its various facets, does not play a vital role in modern microtheory. This is all the more paradoxical since the theory attempts to describe the allocation of resources under a market system – a problem in which the entrepreneur traditionally played a major role.

The question which this study seeks to answer is straightforward: why did the entrepreneur, a fundamental element throughout the history of economic thought, disappear from modern orthodox microeconomics? Of course, in answering this question, a series of related issues must be analyzed, including: (a) a review of the leading roles the entrepreneur is claimed to have played; (b) a determination of exactly when and how the entrepreneur disappeared; and (c) a judgment as to the efficacy of such a change.

Furthermore, the answer to the question is complicated because, as phrased, the query permits several levels of correct responses, each level corresponding to a different meaning of the word 'why'. In an attempt to thoroughly answer the question, a three-level answer will be presented.

1

The first level will describe how the entrepreneur actually disappeared. A review of the histories of entrepreneurial and microeconomic thought is presented in an attempt to give an 'eyewitness account' of the disappearance. The goal is to show that the rapid intellectual changes occurring in the 1930s in microeconomic theory coincided exactly with the disappearance of the entrepreneur from microtheory.

The second level of explanation will focus on the actual reasons for the demise of the entrepreneur. By closely examining modern microeconomic theory (including the theory of the firm), it will be shown that the entrepreneur (in any of the traditional roles) simply cannot exist within the framework of orthodox economic theory.

Finally, and most importantly, the third level of explanation will concentrate on the motivating element behind the elimination of the entrepreneur from current microeconomic theory. The key to this deepest level of explanation lies in consistency – an indispensable attribute of any theoretical structure. Orthodox microeconomic theory is the ultimate fulfilment, in economics, of a perfectly interlocking, self-contained model. The theory of production is composed of three mutually consistent characterizations of the firm's optimization problem: the isoquant, output, and factor market sides. Distribution theory directly results from the solution of the factor-market side maximization problem. Furthermore, in conjunction with consumer theory, the orthodox theory of value is formed. Thus modern orthodox microeconomic theory is a set of internally consistent, nested models, a series of pieces that fit perfectly together to form a grand, unified whole.

Any attempt to introduce the entrepreneur into this theoretical structure destroys the internal consistency of the model. The fundamental explanation for the disappearance of the entrepreneur from microtheory lies in the inability to compromise the consistency requirement. The choice is an 'either-or' proposition; there is no marginal adjustment, no happy medium. The corner solution which modern microtheory has chosen is consistency, and for this reason the entrepreneur has been removed from the orthodox explanatory scheme.

Finally, the reader should note that the explanation advanced here does not have a motivating element behind it – more specifically, there is no particular axe to grind. The purpose of this study is to provide a detailed examination of entrepreneurship and its role throughout the history of microeconomics. Although judgment is passed on the net effects of the elimination of the entrepreneur from orthodox economics, this book is not an addition to the rapidly growing 'what's wrong with economics' library. Instead, it attempts a thorough explanation for an interesting problem in the history of economic thought.

The organization of this book is quite straightforward. The next chapter will review the various roles played by the entrepreneur in the history of economic thought. A framework is presented from which entrepreneurial theories can be categorized and compared. Chapter 3 focuses on the role of the entrepreneur throughout the history of microeconomic theory. The goal here is to show that the entrepreneur did in fact play a major role in mainstream economic theory and did in fact disappear from the orthodox theory.

Thus Chapters 2 and 3 lay the foundation for our question: why did the entrepreneur disappear? The remainder of the book is dedicated to presenting an answer to this question. Chapter 4 contains the first level of explanation – a description of what actually happened. The second level, a more detailed analysis of why the entrepreneur and modern microeconomics could not co-exist, is found in Chapter 5. Finally, the motivation behind the disappearance, the third and most important level of explanation, is discussed in Chapter 6. Judgment of the desirability of the chosen path and some thoughts on the future of microeconomics are reserved for the final chapter.

Note

1 William J. Baumol, 'Entrepreneurship in economic theory', *American Economic Review* 58 (May 1968): 64.

Chapter one

The entrepreneur throughout the history of economic thought

Introduction

For the entrepreneur to disappear from economic theory, he must have been visible at some point in time. In fact, the entrepreneur was more than merely present; he played several fundamental roles in a wide variety of settings. The entrepreneur has been risk-bearer, innovator, industrial leader – the list is almost endless. Entrepreneurship has been used as an explanatory factor in theories designed to analyze growth (and technological change), uncertainty, firm decision-making (and ownership), and the properties of the market system.

It is this extensive and constantly crucial use of the entrepreneur that makes the question of his disappearance from a particular school of economics interesting. This chapter will show just how wide-ranging and how fundamental the entrepreneur has been throughout the history of economic thought.

In order to analyze this main point, a categorization of the many facets of entrepreneurship must be devised. Thus a derivative benefit from the effort to show the important roles the entrepreneur has played is the development of a taxonomy of entrepreneurship. Arranging a mix of different characterizations into a logical framework provides a method with which to analyze research into entrepreneurship. The ultimate objective, however, is to convey the fundamental, indispensable nature of the entrepreneur throughout the history of economic thought.

The key to analyzing the intellectual history of entrepreneurship lies in the framework chosen to present the myriad of characterizations. There are three choices available: categorization by individual author, school, or functional role.

The first two are the traditional means of organization in the history of economic thought.[1] The analysis focuses on the determination of a particular individual's or school's understanding of a

4

given problem. The goal is often a comparison of different points of view, a description of the development of the given problem, or recognition of specific achievements.

None of these, however, is the present objective. There will be no chronological development of the theory of the entrepreneur, primarily because there is no generally accepted theory of entrepreneurship. There is no 'right' answer – only many different ways of viewing the problem. Thus our taxonomy must be determined by the entrepreneur's functional role. This approach will highlight the many varied roles the entrepreneur has played throughout the history of economic thought and avoid issues of priority or correctness.

The entrepreneurial classification scheme presented in this chapter contains four main entries: coordination, arbitrage, innovation, and uncertainty-bearing. In addition, the last category contains three subgroupings: speculation, ownership, and decision-making.

The work of every theorist who has subscribed to a particular view of entrepreneurship will not be reviewed. Instead, a representative work will be chosen and examined. Thus the entrepreneur as coordinator focuses on Jean-Baptiste Say's entrepreneur as combiner of resources. Israel Kirzner's work represents the Austrian theory of the entrepreneur as arbitrageur, an equilibrating agent in a world of imperfect information. The entrepreneur as innovator is captured in Joseph Schumpeter's theory of economic development. Finally, the entrepreneur as uncertainty-bearer is analyzed. The tripartite division is composed of the following representatives: Richard Cantillon (entrepreneur as speculator), F. B. Hawley (entrepreneur as owner of the output), and Frank Knight (entrepreneur as ultimate decision-maker under uncertainty).

It is important to note that neither priority nor any special dominance is bestowed upon those singled out for review. The choices were made based on the clarity of exposition and the specific focus on a particular functional role. For theories in which the entrepreneur plays more than one role, the particular function under consideration will be highlighted.

In addition, the various roles will not be compared or judged. The reader will notice that some descriptions of the entrepreneur's part in the market system are directly contradictory. Although it would be interesting and worthwhile to try to fit the pieces together, this task is outside the scope of this work. Once again, the crucial point to be conveyed is an appreciation for the various dominant roles the entrepreneur has played in the history of economic thought. From Cantillon to Kirzner, economists have investigated the entrepreneur in their quest to gain insight into the market system.

The entrepreneur as coordinator

Jean-Baptiste Say, a French political economist in the early nineteenth century, is most renowned for his 'law of markets'. Say's theory of production, however, contains the germ of all future investigations into the entrepreneur as a coordinating, supervising agent of production.

His major work, *A Treatise on Political Economy*, presents a fairly detailed analysis of the production and distribution of products in a competitive market system.[2] Say's *Cours Complet d'Economie Politique Practique* (1st edition, 1828), also developed a model of production and distribution with a dominant role assigned to entrepreneurship as coordination. In addition, he published an essentially abridged version of the *Treatise* entitled *A Catechism of Political Economy* (translated by John Richter in 1821).

Remarkably, Say's treatment of the entrepreneur went largely unnoticed. Several writers have bemoaned his fellow classical economists' lack of initiative in integrating entrepreneurial considerations into classical economic theory. According to Hebert and Link,

> [Ricardo] failed entirely to pursue Say's suggestion that the entrepreneur is distinguishable from the other agents of production. Smith could not have done so because his work preceded Say's, but Say had formalized the term entrepreneur and given it definition some 14 years before Ricardo's *Principles* appeared. . . . It is noteworthy that in the correspondence between Say and Ricardo, neither the nature nor role of the entrepreneur is once mentioned, the usual discussion focusing instead on the topic of value.[3]

Schumpeter credits Say with presenting economic theory with a fourth agent that hires or 'combines' the others, but notes that the lack of attention resulted in a missed opportunity:

> This could have led – more than it actually did lead – to a clearer perception of the role of the 'capitalist,' who might have been ousted from his position in the center of capitalist industry and put into a more appropriate place among the owners of factors that are being hired.[4]

Koolman presents some possible arguments for the English classical school's neglect of Say's entrepreneur, including: (a) the lack of an entrepreneurial tradition in England; Say's own rationale that (b) the English language was insufficiently developed and (c) the different nature of English law; and (d) the macroeconomic perspective of the English classical school.[5]

In any case, there can be no doubt that Say presented the first, and still quite powerful, view of the entrepreneur as combiner and coordinator of productive services. For this reason, we choose Say's entrepreneur as representative of a coordinating functional role.

The following section presents an overall view of Jean-Baptiste Say's theory of production and distribution. Specific attention is then focused on the entrepreneur as a coordinator – his main functional role in production. The entrepreneur's income, as a special aspect of Say's general distribution theory, is then analyzed in greater detail.

Say's overall theory of production and distribution

Say, following Adam Smith, envisaged three agents of production: 'the means indispensably necessary for the creation of a product: viz. human industry; the capital or value which serves for that purpose; the land and other natural agents which contribute to it.'[6] Capital includes physical capital (tools and implements) and money capital ('advanced' wages). Natural agents include powers 'offered spontaneously by nature: the soil, the air, the rain and the sun, wherein mankind bears no part, but which nevertheless concurs in the creation of the new product'.[7]

Although capital and natural agents are recognized as indispensable, the real key to production lies in labor – human industry. Say analyzes human industry from two distinct viewpoints. First, he categorizes human industry by its actual application in the economy. Thus agricultural industry occurs where human industry is 'limited to the bare collection of natural products' or when man has 'by the cultivation of the earth, and by means of seeds, induced and assisted nature to produce'. The manufacturing industry 'consists in giving to the product of another industry a greater value, by the new forms which we give to it, by the changes which it is made to undergo'. A final means of production occurs 'by buying a product in one place, where it is of less value, and conveying it to another, where it is of greater value. This is the work of Commercial Industry.'[8]

Say's second division of human industry focuses on the functional roles labor performs in the productive process. Once again, he makes a tripartite division, analyzing theory, application, and execution:

> The first step towards the attainment of any specific product, is the study of the laws and course of nature regarding that product. The next step is the application of this knowledge to a useful purpose. The last step is the execution of the manual labour, suggested and pointed out by the two former operations.[9]

All products are produced by the combined efforts of these three functions of human industry. In addition, Say identifies the actors who carry out each particular function:

> One man studies the laws and conduct of nature; that is to say, the philosopher, or man of science, of whose knowledge another avails himself to create useful products; being either agriculturist, manufacturer, or trader; while the third supplies the executive exertion, under the direction of the former two; which third person is the operative workman or labourer.[10]

Say's double tripartite division of human industry in his theory of production is illustrated in Figure 1.1.

The final product can be agricultural, manufactured, or commercial – making the entrepreneur an agriculturist, manufacturer, or trader, respectively. In every case, the entrepreneur plays a key role in the production process, a role which will be further analyzed shortly.

```
Philospher
   (Theory)
ENTREPRENEUR    ===>  HUMAN INDUSTRY    ===>    FINAL PRODUCT
   (Application)
Workman                  "commands"
   (Execution)


                         CAPITAL

                            +

                     NATURAL AGENTS
```

Figure 1.1 Say's production theory

```
FINAL PRODUCT  ===>  WAGES  ===>  ENTREPRENEUR'S WAGE
                                  Philosopher's wage
                                  Workman's wage


                              +


                           INTEREST


                              +


                            RENT
```

Figure 1.2 Say's distribution theory

Say's distribution theory is based on a straightforward extension of supply and demand into the three input markets. The equilibrium wage for each factor of production is determined by the forces of supply and demand. The entrepreneur is the source of demand in the factor market: 'he is the organ of a demand for all the productive agency applicable to this object, and thus, furnishes one of the bases of the value of that agency.'[11] The supply curves of the particular factors are developed in greater detail. Human industry, for example, is supplied in greater or lesser quantities based on the degree of danger or trouble, the regularity or irregularity of the occupation, and the necessary degree of skill or talent.[12]

Thus from the revenue gained by the sale of the product, the various productive agencies are repaid. Note that once again, the entrepreneur plays a crucial role: on the distribution side, he is responsible for paying the productive factors and ensures that total revenue is exactly exhausted (Figure 1.2).

Thus Say's theories of production and distribution are shaped by the classification of various productive factors and their returns. A more detailed analysis of the entrepreneur's role in Say's distribution theory will be conducted after an examination of the entrepreneur as the key factor in production.

The functional role of the entrepreneur in production

Given the three major agencies of production (human industry, capital, and natural agents), we have seen that Say focused on

9

human industry as the key input. A further functional division separated this factor of production into scientist, entrepreneur, and workman. But these are not of equal importance; Say's emphasis clearly lay on the entrepreneur.

Theory and execution are necessary, but it is the entrepreneur who drives the productive process by applying theory and directing execution. Information, in Say's system, is essentially a free good:

> The knowledge of the man of science, indispensable as it is to the development of industry, circulates with great ease and rapidity from one nation to all the rest. For this reason, a nation, in which science is but little cultivated, may nevertheless carry its industry to a very great length by taking advantage of the information derivable from abroad.[13]

The function of the workman was similarly necessary, but downplayed. On the generally low wages for labor, Say wrote, 'Simple, or rough labour may be executed by any man possessed of life and health; wherefore, bare existence is all that is requisite to insure a supply of that class of industry.'[14]

The key to production is the combining function of the entrepreneur. In agricultural, manufacturing, or commercial industry, someone must command the necessary resources and organize the productive process: coordination, supervision, and decision-making are functions filled by the entrepreneur.

> It was further requisite [in addition to knowledge], that a manufacturer should have been found, possessed of the means of reducing the knowledge into practice; who should have at first made himself master of all that was known of that particular branch of industry, and afterwards have accumulated, or procured, the requisite capital, collected artificers and labourers, and assigned to each his respective occupation.[15]

For Say, the entrepreneur's coordinating function is made difficult by the uncertainty of the future. Uncertainty implies that not all applications of knowledge in the production of a product are assured success. The entrepreneur must choose which course of action to take; he must exercise judgment:

> He is called upon to estimate, with tolerable accuracy, the importance of the specific product, the probable amount of the demand, and the means of its production: at one time he must employ a great number of hands; at another buy or

order the raw material, collect labourers, find consumers, and give at all times a rigid attention to order and economy.[16]

In addition, uncertainty implies some measure of disutility from risk-taking must be borne. Say did not emphasize this aspect, merely noting that 'the adventurer may, without any fault of his own, sink his fortune, and in some measure his character'.[17]

By giving the entrepreneur the function of coordination, Say placed the entrepreneur at the crux of the market system. Say viewed the entrepreneur as the center to which many different groups were joined:

> He is the link of communication, as well between the various classes of producers, one with another, as between the producer and consumer. He directs the business of production, and is the centre of many bearings and relations.[18]

Clearly, without this central processing unit, the market could not operate. Decision-making (or judgment) and risk-taking are necessary and dominant operations which the entrepreneur performs in the productive process. But the real key to entrepreneurship is its role in coordinating the desires of different constituencies and keeping the entire system from spinning out of control. As we will see in the next section, Say used the entrepreneur as coordinator to play a central role in the distribution of earnings from the final product to each factor of production.

The entrepreneur's remuneration in Say's theory

For Say, all productive services are remunerated according to the laws of supply and demand. In general, the demand for human industry is a function of product demand: 'When the demand for any product whatever, is very lively, the product agency, through whose means alone it is obtainable, is likewise in brisk demand.'[19] The supply of human industry, in general, depends on the three factors mentioned previously: the degree of irksomeness, the steadiness of the work, and the requisite skill level.

Say then considers the particular problem of the entrepreneur's remuneration. He argues that no new theory is necessary to explain the entrepreneur's wage: 'The price of their labour is regulated, like that of all other objects, by the ratio of the supply, or quantity of that labor thrown into circulation, to the demand or desire for it.'[20]

The demand for entrepreneurship is not explicitly differentiated. We can assume that, like the other factors, it is a simple function of product demand. The supply of entrepreneurship, however, is discussed in greater detail. Say focuses on the limits to supply; there are, in modern language, barriers to entry facing the prospective entrepreneur.

> Not that he must already be rich; for he may work upon borrowed capital; but he must at least be solvent, and have the reputation of intelligence, prudence, probity and regularity; and must be able, by the nature of his connexions, to procure the loan of capital he may happen himself not to possess. These requisites shut out a great many competitors.[21]

Second, entrepreneurial labor requires

> a combination of moral qualities, that are not often found together. Judgement, perseverance, and a knowledge of the world, as well as of business. . . . [The entrepreneur] must possess the art of superintendence and administration. There are a number of obstacles to be surmounted, of anxieties to be repressed, of misfortunes to be repaired, and of expedients to be devised. Those who are not possessed of a combination of these necessary qualities, are unsuccessful in their undertakings; their concerns soon fall to the ground, and their labour is quickly withdrawn from the stock in circulation.[22]

A final limit to the available supply of entrepreneurship is sheer bad luck: 'The adventurer may, without any fault of his own, sink his fortune, and in some measure his character; which is another check to the number of competitors, that also tends to make their agency so much the dearer.'[23]

Thus the entrepreneur's income is a function of financial position (or 'connexions'), various personal qualities, and sheer luck. These limits on supply give the entrepreneur a wage higher than that of the other factors. His total return is composed of a wage for coordinating and decision-making services, interest for capital supplied (see below for a discussion of Say's distinction between entrepreneur and capitalist), and a premium for risk-bearing. Just as the emphasis lay on coordination when analyzing the entrepreneur's productive role, the wage payment is stressed as the dominant component of the entrepreneur's income.

As for how the entrepreneur actually receives his payment, Say utilizes a residual theory of profit. The entrepreneur hires the factors (knowledge and manual labor, capital, and natural agents) and remunerates them for their efforts (wages, interest, and rent, respectively) from the sale of the product. The residual is the entrepreneur's return – in equilibrium, exactly equal to the entrepreneur's wage determined by the forces of supply and demand.

If, after the entrepreneur pays himself the market wage, a surplus still remains, 'the producers of this kind of product become more numerous, and their competition will cause the price of the product to fall'. If revenues cannot cover costs, 'he loses, if he has anything to lose: or if he has nothing, those lose who have given him their confidence'.[24]

Clearly, Say has found yet another place where the entrepreneur must play a central, coordinating role. The entrepreneur is the agent who collects the receipts from the sale of the product and distributes them to the contributing factors of production. According to Say, competition from other entrepreneurs guarantees that no single entrepreneur can 'overpay' himself. Once again we see the entrepreneur at the center of the storm, coordinating the many bits of disjointed pieces into a stable whole.

In analyzing the entrepreneur's productive role, Say was the first to focus on coordination. In his distribution theory, Say had another original contribution: he was the first to explicitly distinguish the entrepreneur from the capitalist.

> To Say it was essential to make this distinction, since in his view it was the entrepreneur who was the active agent in production, and who from his pivotal position in the productive process exercised the most important influence on the distribution of wealth. This was not the role of the capitalist, nor for that matter, that of the landowner, or of the labourer.[25]

This was a distinct break from the classical system of production which was organized around class divisions. The entrepreneur belonged to no particular social class. For Say, entrepreneurship is a distinct functional role that must be performed for production to take place. It can be combined with other functional roles in one person, but the functions and returns can be theoretically separated. Thus Say's typical entrepreneur provided some of his own capital and received an interest payment, but not in his role as entrepreneur, since interest accrued only to the productive agency capital. Importantly, Say's logical, clear analysis allowed him to distinguish correctly between entrepreneur and capitalist.

Jean-Baptiste Say, writing in the early nineteenth century, developed a quite sophisticated theory of production and entrepreneurship. Human industry, capital, and natural agents are the three great agencies of production. However, a heavy emphasis is placed on labor, which is subdivided into theory, application, and execution. The work of application, carried out by the entrepreneur, is seen as the driving force in production. His functions include coordination (the key role), decision-making, and risk-bearing. The entrepreneur's main function is that of a central processing unit: information from a wide variety of sources flows in to the center of the firm where it is processed and where decisions are made. Say argues that this coordinating role is indispensable in the production process.

Say's distribution theory stressed the factors that limit the supply of entrepreneurship (high entry costs, requisite qualities, and random events) which, in turn, accounted for the entrepreneur's usually high returns. In terms of functional role in distribution, it was the entrepreneur who paid the factors their market-determined input prices, keeping the residual as his remuneration. Here we see once again a central place reserved for the entrepreneur. Finally, although the entrepreneur's income includes a return for capital personally supplied, Say argued this was not a return to the entrepreneur *qua* entrepreneur, but as capitalist.

It is not surprising, given Say's background in the business world (he ran a spinning factory), that the entrepreneur would reign supreme in a theory of production and distribution. Say's research led to the elevation of the entrepreneur to a crucial role in the productive and distributive processes (although Say's ideas on entrepreneurship went largely unnoticed by English classical economists, his influence can be seen in the work of future economists such as Leon Walras and Joseph Schumpeter). His work also made clear the separation of the entrepreneur from the capitalist. Say will be remembered for a clear, systematic exposition of entrepreneurship as coordination.

The entrepreneur as arbitrageur

Israel Kirzner has been at the forefront of the recent revival of Austrian economics. A student of Ludwig von Mises, Kirzner developed a theory of the entrepreneur as arbitrageur and equilibrating agent. Because of his Austrian perspective, a proper understanding of Kirzner's entrepreneur requires a review of the Austrian system. We will limit our discussion, however, to the aspects of Austrian theory from which Kirzner draws most heavily.

Kirzner has written several books and many articles. His most important works on entrepreneurship include: *Competition and Entrepreneurship* (1973) and two collections of essays, *Perception,*

Opportunity and Profit (1979) and *Discovery and the Capitalist Process* (1986).

In recent years, a debate has arisen in the Austrian camp over Kirzner's alleged neglect of uncertainty considerations.[26] For our purposes, it is only important to note that there are those who believe uncertainty to be an unnecessary complication (for example, Jack High). Thus the theory of the entrepreneur as arbitrageur lives on. Kirzner's latest writings, perhaps in an attempt to satisfy his critics, include the effects of uncertainty on the entrepreneurial role. However, the basic Kirznerian entrepreneurial role remains unchanged. The prime entrepreneurial characteristic is not uncertainty-bearing – nor anything at all related to uncertainty – but the ability to perceive profit opportunities and act upon them. For this reason, the entrepreneur as arbitrageur deserves its own place in our taxonomy of entrepreneurial theories.

In the next section, some basic tenets of the Austrian tradition are briefly examined, providing the background necessary to understand Kirzner's theory of entrepreneurship. Kirzner's concept of the entrepreneur's functional role in the market system is then discussed. Finally, we examine the nature and function of the entrepreneur's compensation.

The market process and human action

A detailed analysis of Austrian economic thought is outside the scope of our inquiry. A brief review of two fundamental ideas, the market process and human action, are necessary, however, in order to examine Kirzner's entrepreneur as arbitrageur. Orthodox economic theory is useless, Austrians believe, because of its obsession with equilibrium.[27] The focus of modern microeconomic theory is on the values of equilibrium prices and quantities. Comparative statics, the dominant means of analysis, is the simple comparison of old and new equilibrium states after a 'shock' (for example, an exogenous change in tastes or technology). 'In all this the emphasis is on the *prices* and *quantities* and, in particular, on these prices and quantities as they would emerge under equilibrium conditions.'[28] All the while, 'perfect knowledge' is assumed. Disequilibrium occurs if the quantity demanded does not equal the quantity supplied. In such a case, price will adjust until equilibrium is reached.[29]

This is all a very familiar story, but skeptics believe it misses the crucial issues. Critics argue that too many interesting problems are neglected by the analysis of equilibrium states. One such group, the Austrian school led by Friedrich von Hayek and Ludwig von Mises, emphasizes the market system as a process, rather than a determined price-quantity configuration. For the Austrian school, the market is still made up of consumers and producers seeking to make mutually advantageous exchanges. However, an equilibrium solution is far down the road. The goal is to find how disappointments experienced in a disequilibrium market change individual decisions in such a way that there is a tendency toward equilibrium. Austrians believe we should examine

> how the decisions of individual participants in the market interact to generate the market forces which compel changes in prices, outputs, and in methods of production and the allocation of resources. . . . The object of our scientific interest is these alterations themselves, not (except as a matter of subsidiary, intermediate, or even incidental interest) the relationships governing prices and quantities in the equilibrium situation.[30]

After a given exchange is made, the agents may, in light of new information, see a better course of action. New information is gained by exposure to the decisions of others. In the next period, revised decisions will be made, leading to different exchanges.

> In other words, even without changes in the basic data of the market (i. e., in consumer tastes, technological possibilities, and resource availabilities), the decisions made in one period of time generate systematic alterations in the corresponding decisions for the succeeding period. Taken over time, this series of systematic changes in the interconnected network of market decisions constitutes the *market process*.[31]

It should now be clear why the Austrians reject equilibrium analysis: the market process is nonexistent in an equilibrium state. By definition, there is no tendency to change; all expectations are fulfilled.

If the market process is the Austrian answer to equilibrium, then human action is their answer to optimization theory. To the Austrians, a wrong turn was taken when orthodox economics accepted Lionel Robbins' definition of economics as the allocation of scarce resources among competing ends.[32] The key to orthodox economics lies in the assumptions of known means and given ends. Invariably, known variables are chosen to optimize a given objective function (for example, utility or profit). This results in the ceaseless implementation of the equimarginal principle, that is, an arrangement which guarantees an optimum position. Consumers set marginal utility equal to marginal cost when deciding how much of a commodity to buy; producers (be they competitors or monopolists) set marginal revenue equal to marginal cost when deciding how much to produce; workers set marginal income equal to marginal disutility when deciding how many hours to work – the list is almost endless. Any problem of choice that has known variables and objectives can be studied using optimization theory. This, of course, is one of the most powerful features of orthodox economics.

Austrians, however, argue that disequilibrium destroys this neat framework, since the plans of the calculating optimizer are often not realized. For example, given an expected price configuration and cost constraint, the firm chooses an input vector that maximizes output. However, upon arrival at the market, the firm finds surpluses and shortages everywhere, destroying its meticulously laid plans. Obviously, expectations will be revised (even orthodox economic theory tells us this), but the question is, 'How?' Austrians argue that this question is the truly important one, swamping notions of marginal calculations.

The Austrian answer is found in the phrase 'human action'. Mises' great work, *Human Action*, can be viewed as a response to Robbins' definition of the economic problem. Mises 'recognizes that men are not only calculating agents but are also *alert to opportunities*'.[33] Since the world is in a state of disequilibrium, opportunities are constantly being recognized and acted on. In any given period, economic man is more concerned with acquiring information and revising his plans than with determining his optimum market basket. Thus human action is the key to understanding the market process.

The modern Austrian economics revival is a response to the perceived inapplicability of orthodox microeconomic theory. Austrians argue that the equilibrium and allocative decision-making framework badly misses the point: 'The real economic problems in any society arise from the phenomenon of unperceived opportunities.'[34] Thus the better alternative is to focus on the market process – how and why the market tends toward equilibrium. The latter question is explained by a view of economic man focusing on human action – the notion that economic man calculates, but, much more importantly, that he is constantly alert to new opportunities.

The functional role of the entrepreneur

Once we understand Kirzner's Austrian background, the functional role of his entrepreneur is relatively easy to grasp.

In a nutshell, Kirzner places the power of human action on entrepreneurs. They, by constantly being on the alert for new opportunities, drive the market process. Mises argued that everyone possessed the capacity for human action. Kirzner has limited those who are alert to opportunities to a select group, called entrepreneurs, in order to highlight the functional role of entrepreneurship as alertness to opportunity.

For Kirzner, disequilibrium is characterized by ignorance. This ignorance is directly responsible for the existence of profitable opportunities. Expectations are not realized because of mistaken perceptions about the environment. Kirzner gives entrepreneurs the power to reassess previous decisions in the light of new information; that is, they have the ability to learn. For example, suppose a consumer is buying at a higher price than a supplier would be willing to sell. The entrepreneur, by virtue of his alertness to opportunity, can buy at the producer's reservation price and sell to the consumer by undercutting the supplier's retail price, reaping any remaining excess gain. Gradually, competition among entrepreneurs will tend to lower the price to its equilibrium position.

Kirzner, in an attempt to make perfectly clear the functional role of the entrepreneur, defines a 'pure' entrepreneur as an arbitrageur: 'The key point is that *pure* entrepreneurship is exercised only in the *absence* of an initially owned asset. . . . The "pure" entrepreneur observes the opportunity to sell something at a price higher than that at which he can buy it.'[35]

The extension to production changes nothing. The entrepreneur looks for opportunities in which he can generate an excess of total revenues over total cost (including any payments to factors he may own).

The entrepreneur is not a factor of production. He requires no special ability to carry out his function, other than the capacity for perceiving opportunity. Thus the entrepreneur fulfills no coordinating or management role in the productive process. Any special abilities needed to organize factors and choose optimum rates of inputs and outputs are unnecessary.

> All he needs is to discover where buyers have been paying too much and where sellers have been receiving too little and to bridge the gap by offering to buy for a little more and to sell for a little less. To discover these unexploited opportunities requires alertness. Calculation will not help, and economizing and optimizing will not of themselves yield this knowledge.[36]

Then what will? Why do certain people perceive opportunities and others not? Kirzner emphasizes that it is not the acquisition of information per se. There is a distinction between being alert and possessing information – it is the former that is crucial to the market process. Thus the hired expert may possess more knowledge about a particular field than the employer, yet the employer is the entrepreneur. Somehow the employer was able to perceive a profit opportunity and hired the resources (including the expert) to realize the gain. How did the employer, having less knowledge, see what the expert did not?

> We do not clearly understand how entrepreneurs get their flashes of superior foresight. We cannot explain how some men discover what is around the corner before others do. We may certainly explain – on entirely Robbinsian lines – how men explore for oil by carefully weighing alternative ways of spending a limited amount of search resources, but we cannot explain how a prescient entrepreneur realizes before others do that a search for oil may be rewarding.[37]

The entrepreneur is not a factor of production, nor does he possess special knowledge. Clearly, he is neither characterized by resource ownership (that is, a capitalist), nor product ownership. Risk-taking would be an element to be incorporated into the entrepreneurial function, but it is not necessary. In fact, the entrepreneur's only defining characteristic is alertness; his only functional role is that of arbitrageur. In this crucial part, the entrepreneur drives the market toward equilibrium. He is the moving force behind the market process.

Relative to orthodox economic theory, the Austrian story contains a slight, but important distinction. The market is always in disequilibrium, yet entrepreneurial actions generate movements toward equilibrium – an equilibrium that is never reached. Thus there is always a role for the entrepreneur as arbitrageur, endlessly driving the system toward new equilibrium positions.

The reward for entrepreneurship

For Kirzner, entrepreneurial income is defined as a return for arbitrage. The entrepreneur 'proceeds by his alertness to discover and exploit situations in which he is able to sell for high prices that which he can buy for low prices. Pure entrepreneurial profit is the difference between the two sets of prices.'[38]

Yet profit should not be seen as a return to a productive service of some kind: profit is 'something obtainable for nothing at all'.[39] There is no relationship between the profit magnitude and entrepreneurship. It is nonsensical to argue that more entrepreneurship leads to greater profits, since 'entrepreneurship cannot usefully be treated simply as a resource, similar in principle to the other resources available to an economic system'.[40]

It is important to note that the definition of entrepreneurial gain depends very much on one's viewpoint. According to Kirzner, 'the correct theoretical characterization of a particular receipt depends on the character of the decision responsible for that receipt'.[41] A gain earned by selling a resource, for example, may or may not be a profit. If the resource was initially bought in order to be sold at a later date, a profit is earned. If, however, we focus our attention on the mere selling of the resource, the transaction is nothing but the sale of something owned. It is a very real possibility that a particular receipt may be viewed as profit and as something other than profit. The defining characteristic of profit is that it is a result of an entrepreneurial decision to take advantage of a perceived opportunity. Since such a result may be the culmination of a long sequence of decisions, the decision responsible for the gain may be ambiguous. Thus Kirzner quite consistently argues that monopoly gains are an entrepreneurial profit if viewed as the return from the initial capturing of the monopoly position.

To this point, it seems the Austrians view profit as quite inconsequential. After all, it bears no particular relation to entrepreneurship; nor does it 'repay' a productive agency for its services. A more correct way to characterize the Austrian position is that *ex post* profits are relatively meaningless; *ex ante* profit considerations, however, are crucial. Profit is the prime objective of the entrepreneur and the incentive that motivates entrepreneurship.

> We do not know precisely how entrepreneurs experience superior foresight, but we do know, at least in a general way, that entrepreneurial alertness is stimulated by the lure of profits. Alertness to an opportunity rests on the attractiveness of that opportunity and on its ability to be grasped once it has been perceived.[42]

Thus the anticipation of gain, not the realization itself, is the crucial factor. Entrepreneurs, motivated by human action, react to profit opportunities because they anticipate a gain. The larger the prospective gain, the more aware entrepreneurs will be. Profit's role is that of an incentive for entrepreneurial action; distributive considerations are, on the whole, largely ignored.

Finally, it need hardly be said that interest premiums for risk-bearing and the like play no part in Kirzner's entrepreneurial profit theory. Profit is not a functional return or a reward for past performance; it is a call to action or the lure of future success.

In summary, Kirzner views entrepreneurial income as a reward for arbitrage. Profit is defined by the decision that resulted in revenue. If it was an entrepreneurial decision (acting on a perceived opportunity), the revenue is profit; if not (a mere sale of an asset), it is not. But these distinctions are not of primary importance and the distributive aspect of the market process is largely neglected. The real function of profit lies in the lure it presents for entrepreneurs. In this role, profit ensures the working of the market process – the tendency toward equilibrium.

To conclude, Israel Kirzner gains a place in our categorization of functional roles by casting the entrepreneur as an arbitrageur. By this Kirzner does not mean what, to an orthodox economist, would be the 'simple' task of equilibrating supply and demand in a perfect market. Kirzner's story must be told from its proper perspective, that of the Austrian economics tradition where the focus is on disequilibrium and human action. Human action – man's constant alertness to the opportunity to improve his position – drives the market process, the way in which plans are revised and ignorance is lessened.

Kirzner gives the entrepreneur the power of human action, the ability to learn. The entrepreneur's role is to spot opportunities for gain in the disequilibrium environment. The entrepreneur takes advantage of situations where the wrong price prevails (where buyers or sellers are frustrated), where more than one price exists, and where prices of inputs are out of line with their corresponding product prices.

By being alert to opportunities, the entrepreneur in Kirzner's system is the motivating force behind the market process. He is an arbitrageur, an equilibrator, but not in the trite sense of the term. The alertness required is not easily explained and there is an unknown, mystical aura about it.

If the entrepreneur drives the market process, profit drives the entrepreneur. More correctly, it is the expectation or anticipation of gain that stimulates the entrepreneur to action. The entrepreneur remains ever alert to opportunity in the hope that he will be rewarded with a windfall return.

By utilizing the Austrian notions of market process and human action, Kirzner has constructed a viable and appealing account of the entrepreneur as arbitrageur. By constantly closing the gaps resulting from ignorance and lack of information, the entrepreneur is responsible for an ever more smoothly working market. The entrepreneur as arbitrageur plays the crucial role of equilibrating agent and helps explain why markets tend toward equilibrium.

The entrepreneur as innovator

Joseph A. Schumpeter is the originator of one of the most colorful, sweeping theories of entrepreneurship. His entrepreneur is cast as innovator and dynamic agent, the engine of the capitalist economy. For Schumpeter, entrepreneurial actions are the ultimate cause of business cycles and economic development in general.

Over a period of 40 years, Schumpeter was an active and prolific writer. His major works on the theory of the entrepreneur include *The Theory of Economic Development* (originally published in 1911 and translated into English in 1934), *Business Cycles* (1939), and *Capitalism, Socialism and Democracy* (1942).

Unlike Say, Schumpeter's theories have never had any trouble being recognized and discussed. Schneider praises Schumpeter's theory as

> one of the most profound and persuasive of the available analyses of the development process in general and of capitalistic free-market systems in particular. . . . After more than half a century, this work [*The Theory of Economic Development*] has come to be counted – along with Karl Marx's *Capital* – among the foundations which no theory of economic development can ignore.[43]

Schumpeter accepted general equilibrium as the eventual result of a static market system. He had no quarrel with static allocation theorems and the repeated application of optimization theory in a static environment. He argued, however, that the important questions had already been answered and, thus, static theory would not lead to further insights. A shift in problem orientation was needed; the truly interesting problems lay in the process of change. Schumpeter believed the market system has an inherent tendency toward change and that the dynamic attributes of capitalism were its most useful characteristics. Finally, he argued that it is the entrepreneur who plays a crucial role in generating change in a market system. Thus the chain is complete: the hallmark of capitalism is change which, in turn, is caused by the entrepreneur.

The next section will analyze the circular flow of Schumpeter's general equilibrium system. We will focus on the productive and distributive aspects of the economy in a full, competitive general equilibrium. We then turn to an analysis of Schumpeter's theory of entrepreneurship where special attention is focused on the entrepreneur's functional role in the theory of economic

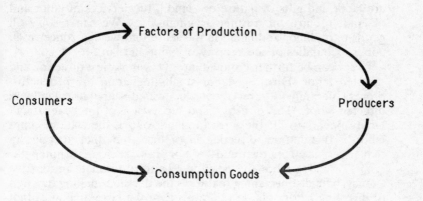

Figure 1.3   The circular flow

development. Finally, the theory of entrepreneurial profit – a result of development – is discussed in detail.

The circular flow

Schumpeter examines the phenomenon of economic development by contrasting a progressive with a non-developing economy. Essentially, Schumpeter's exposition of the stationary state, the circular flow, is a non-mathematical recounting of a Walrasian general equilibrium. He does include an extra dimension, the circular flow through time (that is, a dynamic general equilibrium), in order to compare a static with a dynamic economy.

The static general equilibrium model is built on the exchange of goods for productive services between producers and consumers. In a static sense, the circular flow is depicted in Figure 1.3.

All goods and services in the system are classified, following Menger, according to their 'order'. First-order goods are directly used by the consumer, that is, consumption goods. Second-order goods are 'goods from combinations of which consumer goods immediately originate . . . and so on, in continually higher and more remote orders'.[44] A good is ranked in the highest of the orders in which it ever appears: 'Accordingly labor is, for example, a good of the highest order, because labor enters at the very beginning of all production, although it is also to be found at all other stages'.[45]

Ascending the hierarchy of goods, the ultimate elements in production will eventually be found. 'That these ultimate elements

23

are labor and gifts of nature or "land", the services of labor and of land, requires no further argument. . . . We can resolve all goods into "labor and land" in the sense that we can conceive all goods as bundles of the services of labor and land.'[46]

Labor can be further grouped into two categories: directing and directed labor. Directing labor stands higher in the productive process hierarchy; it directs, coordinates, and supervises land and directed labor. 'This direction and supervision of the "executing" labor appears to lift the directing labor out of the class of other labor.'[47] In addition, directing labor 'has something creative in that it sets itself its own ends'.[48] For these reasons, Schumpeter grants directing labor the position of a third ultimate productive agency. The distinguishing feature is the decision-making function of directing labor. The key, however, in the circular flow is that these decisions have been made the same way countless times before.

The director must make some resolutions and independently decide some questions, but he does so on the basis of past learning and experience. In the circular flow, no new means of reaching an end are attempted.

> [The director] acts, not on the basis of the prevailing conditions of things, but much more according to certain symptoms of which he had learned to take heed, especially of the tendencies immediately showing in the demand of his customers. And to these tendencies he yields step by step, so that only elements of minor significance can ordinarily be unknown to him.[49]

If directing labor, directed labor, and land are the ultimate productive factors, then the next question is: 'On what basis does their remuneration depend?' Schumpeter follows the straight marginal productivity imputation theory. Productive services receive value from the value of the product. A given individual unit of a factor receives an income based on the product's value and the factor's marginal productivity. Furthermore, in a perfectly competitive circular flow, the factors are guaranteed the full return of the value of the total product. In other words, factor price payments equal total revenues. The theory of production and distribution in the circular flow can be more fully explained by Figure 1.4.

Once again, the key to understanding Schumpeter's concept of general equilibrium or the circular flow lies in the repetitive, routine nature of decision-making. Consumers buy roughly the same goods, in the same quantities, the same way; producers make the same output, in the same quantities, the same way.

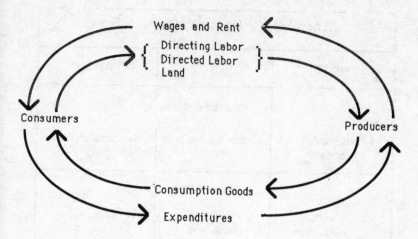

Figure 1.4 The full circular flow

Consumers make the same expenditures and producers pay the same wages and rents. The system is marked by equilibrium, that is, no tendency to change.

Schumpeter then turns to the question of time. He admits that consumption goods in general are not produced directly by the ultimate productive factors. Typically, producer goods play an intermediary role in the productive process. Thus consumption goods require two economic periods for their completion.

Without becoming deeply involved in a detailed analysis, Schumpeter's basic problem is the existence of current productive power being exchanged for future consumption goods. The classical economists solved this problem by applying the notion of 'advanced' wages. This creates another necessary agency in production, usually referred to as capital. Schumpeter argues, however, that the circular flow is timeless. In period *t*, the consumer receives consumption goods produced in period *t* in exchange for productive services. Some of these services are used to make producer goods for period *t*+1; the rest are used in conjunction with producer goods from *t*–1 to make consumption goods for period *t*. In the next period, the process repeats itself, as shown in Table 1.1. Thus, Schumpeter ingeniously sidesteps the problem of time in the productive process.

Therefore, workers and landlords always exchange their productive services for present consumption goods only, whether the former are employed directly or only indirectly in the production of consumption goods. There is no necessity for them to exchange

Schumpeter's Dynamic Circular Flow		
Period t-1	Period t	Period t+1
	CONSUMPTION	
t-1 consumption goods	t consumption goods	t+1 consumption goods
	PRODUCTION	
t-1 consumption goods from t-1 productive services and t-2 producer goods	t consumption goods from t productive services and t-1 producer goods	t+1 consumption goods from t+1 productive services and t producer goods
t-1 producer goods from t-1 productive services	t producer goods from t productive services	t+1 producer goods from t+1 productive services

Table 1.1 Schumpeter's circular flow over time

their services of labor and land for future goods, for promises of future consumption goods, or to apply for any 'advances' of present consumption goods. It is simply a matter of exchange, and not of credit transactions. The element of time plays no part. All products are only products and nothing more.[50]

Using his notion of a timeless yet moving circular flow, Schumpeter argues that the notion of a capital fund is superfluous. By logical extension, in the circular flow, there is no return to capital: 'in each period all the consumption goods on hand will go to the services of labor and land employed in this period; hence all incomes are absorbed under the title of wages or rent of natural agents.'[51]

The circular flow is a self-perpetuating mechanism. Individual

26

businesses are places where products are made and revenues are divided among the productive services. The necessary requirements for production, in the ultimate sense, are directed labor, land, and directing labor (which serves to combine the other two). The key is that the function of directing labor 'is performed in every period mechanically as it were, of its own accord, without requiring a personal element distinguishable from superintendence and similar things'.[52] Distribution of income is based on marginal utility (product value) and marginal productivity considerations. Against this backdrop, Schumpeter introduces the entrepreneur as the dynamic agent in development. To the examination of this process, we now turn.

The theory of economic development

Given an understanding of the circular flow, Schumpeter's theory of economic development is straightforward. Development is defined as endogenous change – wars, acts of God, and the like are excluded. In addition, 'mere growth' (the increase of population and wealth) is not development.

Schumpeter defines development in terms of radical disturbance.

> It is spontaneous and discontinuous change in the channels of the flow, disturbance of equilibrium, which forever alters and displaces the equilibrium state previously existing. Our theory of development is nothing but a treatment of this phenomenon and the processes incident to it.[53]

For Schumpeter, development is characterized by a variety of internal changes.

> This concept covers the following five cases: (1) The introduction of a new good – that is one with which consumers are not yet familiar – or of a new quality of a good. (2) The introduction of a new method of production, that is one not yet tested by experience in the branch of manufacture concerned, which need by no means be founded upon a discovery scientifically new, and can also exist in a new way of handling a commodity commercially. (3) The opening of a new market, that is a market into which the particular branch of manufacture of the country in question has not previously entered, whether or not this market has existed before. (4) The conquest of a new source of supply of raw materials or half-manufactured goods, again irrespective of whether this

source already exists or whether it has first to be created. (5) The carrying out of the new organization of any industry, like the creation of a monopoly position (for example through trustification) or the breaking up of a monopoly position.[54]

The key phrase in understanding Schumpeter's theory of economic development is 'new combination', that is, innovation. It is the new good, new method of production, new market, new source, or new organization that defines economic development. The new combination is not defined in terms of slight, incremental change, but as radical, discontinuous breaks from the past. New combinations occur regardless of institutional make-up. Under the free market system, it is the entrepreneur who carries out new combinations, he 'is the key figure and champion of any economic development'.[55]

Established firms are neither necessarily nor typically the bearers of change. In addition, innovation never takes place by acquiring idle productive factors. Currently employed factors must be induced away from their present employment. Therefore, the carrying out of new combinations implies command over means of production, which raises the problem of procurement of these means. Entrepreneurs are aided in this endeavor by the banker (or capitalist) who provides credit.

> The essential function of credit in our sense consists in enabling the entrepreneur to withdraw the producer's goods which he needs from their previous employments, by exercising a demand for them, and thereby to force the economic system into new channels.[56]

Obviously, the capitalist is unnecessary if the entrepreneur possesses or can acquire the necessary means independently. But this is not an integral part of the entrepreneurial role, nor the 'fundamentally interesting case'.

Given the circular flow, the entrepreneur, and credit, the process of development can be traced. Schumpeter focuses on the effects of the shock of carrying out a new combination, termed 'creative destruction' in later work. Unfortunately, a detailed analysis of Schumpeter's theory is outside the scope of this work. Suffice it to say that the crucial point is the wavelike motion of this process: innovations come in bunches or 'swarms'. The first entrepreneur smooths the road and is followed by 'imitators' who carry the 'boom' further. Eventually, due to a variety of factors, the wave dies and the system falls into a recession, then settles into a new equilibrium. Thus the entrepreneur in his innovating role is the cause of business cycles and economic development.

It must be emphasized that although direction and supervision are necessary, it is the direction and supervision of new combinations that characterize the entrepreneur's function. Schumpeter argues that previous definitions of the entrepreneurial role focusing on superintendence and combination of factors are inadequate at best, and often lead to error. 'Mere management', decision-making based on established grounds, is not part of the entrepreneurial function. It fails to 'bring out what we consider to be the salient point and the only one which specifically distinguishes entrepreneurial from other activities' – that is, the carrying out of a new combination.[57] In the circular flow, decisions are made in a routine manner. It is the very special function of the entrepreneur to exude leadership in his path-breaking role. Leadership in the circular flow is superfluous. We speak of the entrepreneurial function because it is a special kind of supervising, coordinating function; it is supervision and coordination over new, untried methods.

The entrepreneur, in exercising his function, is met with severe obstacles. Outside the circular flow, he is forced to act in areas where previous experience is no guide.

> Here the success of everything depends upon intuition, the capacity of seeing things in a way which afterwards proves to be true, even though it cannot be established at the moment, and of grasping the essential fact, discarding the unessential, even though one can give no account of the principles by which this is done.[58]

Second, there is an inherent, instinctive resistance to change. By human nature, we are reluctant to try something new even if the change in itself presents no particular difficulties.

> A new and another kind of effort of will is therefore necessary in order to wrest, amidst the work and care of the daily round, scope and time for conceiving and working out the new combination and to bring oneself to look upon it as a real possibility and not merely as a day-dream.[59]

Finally, the social environment surrounding the prospective entrepreneur has a similar reaction against any change. To varying degrees, in all cultures, 'any deviating conduct by a member of a social group is condemned'.[60] Thus the entrepreneur must overcome the difficulty of finding the necessary cooperation.

The ideas that Schumpeter tries to convey were expressed in a different time and place by no less than Niccolo Machiavelli. In *The Prince*, the well-known Italian schemer and power-broker writes:

> It must be considered that there is nothing more difficult to carry out, nor more doubtful of success, nor more dangerous to handle, than to initiate a new order of things. For the reformer has enemies in all those who profit by the old order, and only lukewarm defenders in those who profit by the new order, this lukewarmness arising . . . partly from the incredulity of mankind, who do not truly believe in anything new until they have had actual experience of it.[61]

For these reasons, the successful entrepreneur is rare indeed. Not only is the environment hostile, but the number of successful entrepreneurs is further limited by the personal qualities required: the desire 'to found a private kingdom, . . . the will to conquer, . . . the joy of creating, of getting things done, or simply exercising one's energy and ingenuity'.[62] Note that entrepreneurship is not something done on rational utility-maximizing grounds. Schumpeter's entrepreneur is a creature driven by instinctive and non-calculating motives.

Before concluding our review of what Schumpeter's entrepreneur is, we must analyze what he is not. The entrepreneur is most certainly not a risk-bearer: 'Risk obviously always falls on the owner of the means of production or of the money-capital which was paid for them, hence never on the entrepreneur as such.'[63] The entrepreneur, once again, is not just anyone who supervises, coordinates, or manages. The key is doing these things in a novel fashion. The entrepreneur is also to be distinguished from the inventor. Although invention must precede innovation, it is the actual implementation – the carrying out – of new combinations that characterizes the entrepreneur's role. Finally, the entrepreneur cannot be defined by his position in the class hierarchy. His is a purely functional role devoid of any class connotation.[64]

By contrasting a developing economy against the backdrop of the circular flow, Schumpeter is able to define precisely the entrepreneurial function. He basically refines Say's notion of direction and coordination by insisting on a further requirement: the carrying out of new combinations. This is the ultimate cause of economic development.

Entrepreneurial profit

Once again, Schumpeter uses the circular flow as a tool to distinguish a particular phenomenon. In this case, entrepreneurial gain or profit is analyzed. In the circular flow, the ultimate factors (directing and directed labor and land) received the total value product (in the form of wages and rent). Factor returns were exactly determined by marginal utility and marginal productivity considerations. No surplus – profit – remained; heads of firms received 'wages of management'. In a developing economy, however, new combinations lead to profit.

'Profit' is defined simply as 'a surplus over costs. . . . It is the difference between receipts and outlays in a business.'[65] Outlays include the direct or indirect payments necessary to hire productive services, for example wages, rents, and interest (including payments for services owned by the entrepreneur in his role as laborer, landowner, or capitalist). For example, the introduction of a new combination in production implies that the new method is more advantageous than the old. Typically, the innovation results in a lower unit cost, leading to a positive difference between the prevailing equilibrium price and the new lower average cost.

Profit is the signal to imitators that above normal gains can be made. Entry and competition eventually erode the initial profit position and a new equilibrium position is reached. The key is that, although temporary, profit is a net gain, that is, 'it is not absorbed by the value of any cost factor through a process of Imputation'.[66] Profit is a true surplus, an excess over the sum of the factor payments. The profit falls to those who introduced the new combination. (Schumpeter makes clear, however, that this need not be the case. In a non-exchange or command economy, profit can be channeled away from the entrepreneur. He also discusses the ramifications this has for taxation under a market system – see below.)

What exactly does the entrepreneur contribute to the productive process?

> Only the will and the action: not concrete goods, for they bought these – either from others or from themselves; not the purchasing power with which they bought, for they borrowed this – from others or, if we also take account of acquisition in earlier periods, from themselves. And what have they done? They have not accumulated any kind of goods, they have created no original means of production, but have employed existing means of production differently, more

31

appropriately, more advantageously. They have 'carried out new combinations.' They are entrepreneurs. And their profit, the surplus, to which no liability corresponds, is an entrepreneurial profit.[67]

The rise of entrepreneurial profit can occur by any of the five means of innovation: the creation of a new good, the introduction of a new method of production, the opening of a new market, the conquest of a new source of raw materials, or the reorganization of an industry. The entrepreneur's gain is easily distinguished from the capitalist's return. The latter's reward is interest payments, including a premium for risk-bearing. The entrepreneur contributes no concrete goods or money capital *qua* entrepreneur. It is the capitalist who must bear the brunt of failure and he is rewarded accordingly. Further, profit is not a rent. For example, the initial act of monopolistic reorganization of an industry is entrepreneurial in nature and its reward is a profit. However, once it is running smoothly, any further surplus must be 'imputed to those natural or social forces upon which the monopoly position rests – it has become monopoly revenue'.[68]

Profit has no tendency to be equalized, except at zero in the circular flow. It is not wages of management and it is not a return to 'exploitation'. Neither, on the other hand, is it a simple residuum: profit expresses the value of the entrepreneur's contribution in the productive process just as wages measure what the worker produces. 'However, while wages are determined according to the marginal productivity of labor, profit is a striking exception to this law: the problem of profit lies precisely in the fact that the laws of cost and of marginal productivity seem to exclude it.'[69] The size of profit, therefore, is not determined (as are wages) such that it just suffices to call forth the necessary quantity of entrepreneurial services. The total profit realized may be, and often is, greatly disproportionate to the needed amount. Thus profits could conceivably be taxed without impairing the market process. In addition, it explains why the industrial manager, who often fills the entrepreneurial role, can be adequately remunerated with a small share of the profit.

Schumpeter's entrepreneurial profit theory emphasizes the need for new combinations in the generation of profit. There is no surplus in the circular flow. It is only through innovation that profit arises and through imitation and competition that it disappears. Profit is a return to the entrepreneurial role, but no law as to its magnitude can be tolerably accepted. The mixing of profit and interest has led to much confusion, but it is clear, in the

Schumpeterian system, that the two are separate and bear no special relationship to one another.

To conclude our discussion, Schumpeter's entrepreneurial theory, at its most fundamental level, is not difficult to understand. By contrasting the circular flow (characterized by the absence of entrepreneurship and profit) with development (defined by new combinations and the resulting profit), he is able to clearly and explicitly define the entrepreneurial role and its return.

Schumpeter's entrepreneur is the functional agent who carries out new combinations. He breaks out of established patterns, thereby disrupting the circular flow. This process of creative destruction is the means by which an economy develops. The key lies not in decision-making per se, but in decision-making that results in new combinations (new goods, different productive processes, and the like). In carrying out new combinations the entrepreneur generates profits, a surplus of receipts over outlays. Under a free market system, he reaps his excess, paying the remaining factors their respective value of the marginal products. The size of profits, as in Kirzner's theory, bears no discernible relationship to the entrepreneurial role.

Schumpeter searched for the cause of systematic, endogenous change in market economies. In the process of explaining the business cycle, Schumpeter found an entire theory of economic development. At the core of the Schumpeterian explanatory scheme lies the entrepreneur, inducing change and reactions from imitators. A single agent, the entrepreneur, is the key element in Schumpeter's theory of economic development.

The entrepreneur as uncertainty-bearer

The theories of entrepreneurship discussed above share a common characteristic: any uncertainty inherent in the economic environment is very much downplayed. Say focuses on coordination, Krizner stresses arbitrage, and Schumpeter emphasizes innovation. Though there are important distinctions drawn between equilibrium and disequilibrium, uncertainty is not a crucial issue. In the history of entrepreneurial thought, however, perhaps the most common entrepreneurial role has been that of uncertainty-bearer. This section will examine three theories of entrepreneurship that make uncertainty-bearing the distinguishing feature of enterpreneurship.

The introduction of uncertainty has several ramifications. Theorists cast the entrepreneur's main function according to a subjective interpretation of the most important effect of an uncertain environment. The earliest entrepreneurial theory, credited to Richard Cantillon, presents the entrepreneur as speculator. Cantillon stressed the need to overcome uncertainty for market exchanges to take place. Frederick Hawley perceived the most important impact of uncertainty to be manifested through the ownership of the product. Thus his entrepreneur performs the economic function of uncertainty-bearing through product ownership. Finally, Frank Knight sees decision-making when consequences are unforeseeable as the crucial function in an uncertain environment – a function performed by the entrepreneur.

These theories all have uncertainty at their core. Without an uncertain environment, the entrepreneur would disappear. This is untrue of the earlier theories discussed and is the basis, therefore, for our categorization of uncertainty-bearing as a fourth main entrepreneurial function. In discussing the entrepreneur as uncertainty-bearer, there is no one theory representative of the different roles the entrepreneur may play in an environment characterized by uncertainty. Therefore we make a further division and analyze in turn the entrepreneur as speculator (Cantillon), product owner (Hawley), and decision-maker (Knight).

The organization of this section is made simpler because a full review of each author's economic theory is not needed. Cantillon's production theory is unimportant for our purposes; Hawley and Knight are neoclassical marginalists, roughly subscribing to Schumpeter's equilibrium view (the circular flow). Thus there is no need to review their overall theories of production and distribution. Each section will simply be divided into an examination of the entrepreneur's productive function and his remuneration.

The entrepreneur as speculator

Richard Cantillon, a pre-Physiocratic French economist, focused on the entrepreneur's role in a free market system. The entrepreneur (or 'undertaker'' in Henry Higgs' 1931 translation of the *Essai sur la Nature du Commerce en General*, Cantillon's only surviving work) conducts all of the exchanges in the market, buying from producers and selling to consumers. By performing this function, he leads the market toward equilibrium. But he is more than a mere arbitrageur (buying low and selling high) because of the presence of uncertainty. The entrepreneur, in conducting his transactions, buys at a certain price and sells at an uncertain one. He is a speculator.

Cantillon's entrepreneur as speculator is the key to the market system because of his willingness to bear risk. Risk is inherent in competition and its dangers are clear: 'every day one sees some of them [entrepreneurs] become bankrupt.'[70] Though many fail, those who survive drive the market toward equilibrium. Entrepreneurs respond to profit opportunities, bringing together the quantities demanded and supplied. If profits are made, there is entry; losses lead to exit. Without the entrepreneurial element, no exchanges would take place.

Cantillon's income distribution theory is very simple: the entrepreneur receives any and all profit (the excess of realized selling price over the certain cost). Cantillon uses a risk theory of profit as a means to identify entrepreneurship. Any agent, laborer, landlord, or capitalist who receives an uncertain income is an entrepreneur. The farmer, for example, who pays a fixed sum for the productive factors (land, labor, and raw materials) in return for an uncertain profit, is an entrepreneur. 'The price of the Farmer's produce depends naturally upon these unforeseen circumstances ["the weather . . . the demand . . . the number of births and deaths"], and consequently he conducts the enterprise of his farm at an uncertainty.'[71] Similarly the 'Carrier', who buys the farmer's produce and transports it to the city, is an entrepreneur by virtue of his uncertain return.

[The Carriers] bind themselves to pay the Farmer a fixed price for his produce, that of the market price of the day, to get in the City an uncertain price which should however defray the cost of carriage and leave them a profit. But the daily variation in the price of produce in the City, though not considerable, makes their profit uncertain.[72]

Cantillon, tracing the various exchanges that are made as the product reaches the consumer, repeatedly points out the distinguishing feature of entrepreneurship, the uncertain return. Wholesalers buy from carriers at a certain price and sell to retailers at an uncertain price. Retailers buy from wholesalers at a certain price and sell to consumers at an uncertain price. Farmers, carriers, wholesalers, and retailers are all entrepreneurs.

Cantillon, in fact, extends his definition to cover some unlikely 'entrepreneurs'. Anyone earning an uncertain income is an entrepreneur, 'whether they set up with a capital to conduct their enterprise, or are Undertakers of their own labour without capital . . . the Beggars even and the Robbers are Undertakers of this class.'[73]

Anyone who receives a fixed income cannot be, by definition, an entrepreneur; they are 'hired people'. Cantillon warns that the absolute magnitude of the fixed wage is irrelevant: 'The General who has his pay, the Courtier his pension and the Domestic servant who has wages all fall into this last class [hired people].'[74]

Cantillon's entrepreneur is a crucial part of the market system, buying at a fixed price and selling at an uncertain one. The willingness to do this allows exchange to take place. Furthermore, the responsiveness to profit opportunities drives the market toward equilibrium. Cantillon's distribution theory focuses entirely on the type of income earned. Receipt of an uncertain return is the identifying feature of the entrepreneur.

By the middle of the eighteenth century, Richard Cantillon had presented the first theory of entrepreneurship, casting the entrepreneur as a speculator in an uncertain environment. Cantillon's focus on uncertainty was not to be a unique view of the entrepreneurial role and his influence on future economists can be seen clearly, for example, in the work of Jean-Baptiste Say.

The entrepreneur as owner

Frederick Barnard Hawley, a prominent American economist, published several articles on entrepreneurship in the *Quarterly Journal of Economics* during the early 1900s. His main ideas on the topic are contained in *Enterprise and the Productive Process* (written in 1907).

Hawley accepted the orthodox production theory (land, labor, and capital as the three great agencies of production), but argued that a particularly crucial element, enterprise, was missing. Hawley accepted labor as the physical or mental efforts provided by man; capital as abstinence or waiting; and land as natural agents provided by nature. He added the function of enterprise as 'the assumption of responsibility in industrial undertakings'.[75]

Hawley then makes a fundamental division: the three orthodox factors are classified as 'means of production'; enterprise is the 'cause or purpose' of production.[76] In a very real sense, Hawley superimposed a dominant element, enterprise, over the orthodox theory of production. Enterprise is not a productive factor or means, but rather a motivational force.

Hawley's basis for distinguishing between land, labor, and capital, on the one hand, and enterprise, on the other, lies in the hierarchical nature of the productive process. The key is that the landowner, laborer, and capitalist look to the enterpriser for direction. The enterpriser commences the productive process:

'Enterprise is the source of all economic activity, as well as of all individualistic and social activities.'[77]

But the adoption of the entrepreneurial role carries with it a cost – the assumption of responsibility. In an uncertain environment, the enterpriser motivates production and becomes the responsible owner of the product. By his ownership, he assumes the responsibility of the use and employment of the means of production and the sale of the product.

The enterpriser who first creates the product is the only true productive agent; land, labor, and capital are means to an end designated by the enterpriser: 'Just as it is the man who pays for having it dug who digs the ditch, and not the owner of the land or of the spade or of the muscular force employed.'[78]

Hawley emphasizes repeatedly that coordination is not the key element in the enterpriser's function. He criticizes the perceived orthodoxy for casting the entrepreneur as a coordinator and placing him on equal footing with the other means of production. Hawley argues that the enterpriser

> is only a co-ordinator in the sense that he directs co-ordination for his own benefit, or rather is co-ordinated for. He is the principal, they [land, labor, and capital] are the agents. Co-ordinations . . . are only the means by which he attains his end, which is to subject himself to the benefits of ownership with its attendant responsibilities.[79]

Hawley's conception of the enterpriser is an attempt to find the seat of power in the productive process. Productive factors are mere tools; enterprise is the head – figuratively and functionally – of the productive process.

> Subject to the limitation that he must produce what consumers will pay him for at a remunerative rate, the enterpriser is the sole arbiter as to the method and direction of production. The landlord, as such, has nothing at all to say about the crops that the renting farmer will raise; or the capitalist, as such, about how his capital shall be invested; or the laborer, as such, about what he shall work at. The direction of production – what shall be produced, how much of it, and by what methods – lies wholly with the enterpriser, who will allow the landlords, capitalists, and the labourers only what prevailing conditions enforce.[80]

Thus Hawley's enterpriser has a key function in the productive process: using the means of production at his disposal, he decides what to do. His power is derived from his ownership rights. He owns (or if he rents, he assumes responsibility for) the means of production. Any product created is therefore property of the enterpriser. By virtue of his ownership rights, he can dispose and direct the means under his control or the final product as he sees fit. However, the enterpriser operates in a world of uncertainty. If the product is destroyed, if an improved good steals his customers, or any of a variety of unforeseen events ruin the enterprise, it is the enterpriser as responsible owner who bears the burden.

Hawley's distribution theory grants wages to labor, interest to capital, and rent to land according to supply and demand considerations. The enterpriser is the distributive agent, paying the means of production their fixed returns. As for the enterpriser himself, he is the claimant of profits – the uncertain residual income. Profits are a return to ownership, a return for bearing the attendant risks and responsibilities. Profit 'is the distinct result, incentive to, and reward of the involved assumption of responsibility'.[81]

The role of profit is the usual one of incentive and signal: 'Profit is the sole inducement to every volitional human thought or action.'[82] Large profits will induce entry; losses lead to exit. In discussing his theory of distribution, Hawley stresses again the difference between enterprise and coordination, arguing that profit is not a return for the function of coordination. Profit can only be gained by the one who has production take place for his benefit, by he who bears the responsibility of the results. 'It is only when the co-ordinator subjects himself to the result of his own co-ordination, or of the co-ordination of others, that he becomes the recipient of profits.'[83]

Hawley casts the entrepreneur as a motivational and uncertainty-bearing element, not a factor of production. The factors, or means, of production are guided by the enterpriser. This is not to say the crucial role is coordination, for a mere coordinator can be hired and paid a fixed wage. The enterpriser is a guide in the sense of choosing what product will be produced; he holds the seat of power in the productive process. The entrepreneur's power is derived from his willingness to be the ultimately responsible agent in the productive process. The means of production are guaranteed their fixed returns; the enterpriser receives an uncertain residual. Hawley's risk theory of profit highlights his conception of the entrepreneur as responsible owner. In a nutshell, the enterpriser makes the grand decisions, answers to no one (except, indirectly, to the consumers) and bears the gain or loss of his endeavors. Once again, yet for another different reason, the entrepreneur is the key to the productive process.

The entrepreneur as decision-maker

Frank H. Knight focused on the responsible decision-making function in an uncertain environment. Although a prolific writer throughout his career, the fundamentals of his theory of entrepreneurship can be found in his doctoral dissertation, published in 1921, *Risk, Uncertainty and Profit*.

Knight followed Schumpeter's exposition, first describing the world in its ideal state of general equilibrium. Then, with the introduction of uncertainty, the entrepreneur's function becomes the principle element in production and distribution.

For Knight, the crucial 'heroic' assumption of orthodox production theory lies in 'the assumption of practical omniscience on the part of every member of the competitive system'.[84] This assumption of perfect knowledge or perfect information reduces the productive process to a mechanical model. Land (natural agents), labor (worker and 'mere manager') and capital (advances to the factors during the period of production) combine to make a product. The price system is the grand allocator of resources to their most productive uses and arbiter of which products are produced. In fact, the price system answers all the questions an economic system must confront: how, what, where, and when products are produced and distributed.

The productive factors are on an equal footing; management plays no special role. Managers are undoubtedly necessary to coordinate resources, 'but under conditions of perfect knowledge and certainty such functionaries would be laborers merely, performing a purely routine function, without responsibility of any sort, on a level with men engaged in mechanical operations'.[85]

It is important to note that in such an ideal state, pure profit is nonexistent. Each factor, including management, will receive a fixed return based on its respective value of the marginal product. Any deviation from the exact equality of revenues and costs (the sum of the factor payments) leads to instantaneous adjustment.

Knight then introduces the crucial element of uncertainty. He carefully distinguishes, however, between risk and uncertainty. Risk is defined as a random event with a known distribution. Uncertainty is randomness in which the distribution of probabilities is *completely* unknown. This distinction is the basis of a critique against previous risk theories of profit (including Hawley's). Randomness per se is not critical. If the chances of an event occurring are known, they can be accounted for (for example, through insurance) and the system will function exactly as

39

before. Managers will routinely calculate expected values and receive fixed returns; pure profit will remain nonexistent.

Uncertainty, however, tremendously changes the workings of the system. There is no basis on which to proceed, yet proceed we do. Someone must take the responsibility of decision-making in such an environment. A new productive agent arises – the entrepreneur. Uncertainty forces decisions to be made under ignorance; actions are based on opinion rather than knowledge. 'With uncertainty present, doing things, the actual execution of activity, becomes in a real sense a secondary part of life; the primary problem or function is deciding what to do and how to do it.'[86] Thus the entrepreneur usurps one of the functions of the price system by determining what products are produced. It is the functional role of the entrepreneur to forecast consumers' wants and direct production toward those perceived wants. It is the presence of uncertainty that implies a role for responsible decision-making. The decisions taken and actions carried out are not guaranteed success; the possibility of gain is accompanied by a more probable chance of loss.

At its most fundamental level, Knight's entrepreneurial theory is simply based on the realization that someone must decide what to do and be responsible for that decision. The crucial nature of this function lies in the fact that the entrepreneur never really knows in advance if his plans and expectations are correct.

The entrepreneur performs his responsible decision-making function by forecasting demand and estimating the factors' marginal productivities. On the basis of their anticipated value of the marginal product, the entrepreneur pays the factors a contractual wage. Production proceeds and the product is distributed. Any divergence between the actual and anticipated value of the marginal product is borne by the entrepreneur. Thus the entrepreneur bears uncertainty, taking the chances and simultaneously shielding those who are unwilling to gamble from the effect of an uncertain environment. Any decision taken involving responsibility for possible error is an entrepreneurial decision.

Knight extends his entrepreneurial theory, discussing how one becomes an entrepreneur, the entrepreneur in the corporation, and the like. Unfortunately, a detailed examination of these issues is beyond the scope of this work. An important point, however, which will further emphasize the entrepreneur's functional role, is Knight's discussion of delegation in the modern corporation. The true entrepreneur is the one who, even if he did not make a particular decision, is responsible for the decision.

The responsible decision is not the concrete ordering of policy, but ordering an orderer as a 'laborer' to order it. And this final responsibility necessarily takes the consequences of its decisions . . . the crucial decision is the selection of men to make decisions.[87]

Thus Knight's entrepreneur is more than a manager or actual productive service. He keys the productive process by deciding, in an uncertain environment, what and how to produce. He is entrepreneur by virtue of his willingness to accept the results of a particular endeavor.

Knight's theory of distribution revolves around his uncertainty theory of profits. The productive services hired by the entrepreneur receive an imputed contractual return based on their anticipated value of the marginal product. The entrepreneur as responsible decision-maker receives the 'pure profit' – the residual difference between realized revenues and estimated (paid) costs. Clearly, uncertainty is a necessary condition for the existence of pure profits.

The entrepreneur receives pure profit as a return for responsible decision-making and insuring factor owners a certain income. Pure profits, however, are not an imputed return.[88] Like Kirzner and Schumpeter, Knight denies any relationship between pure profit and entrepreneurial services. The magnitude of pure profits is determined by the competition of rival entrepreneurs and non-entrepreneurs. Pure profits are high if the entrepreneur is not forced to pay as much as he could for the factor services. For Knight, profits act as a signal, not only in influencing entry and exit, but also in showing the factors they can get a greater return. Thus Knightian pure profits are squeezed from several directions.

Knight's theory of entrepreneurship focuses on the entrepreneur's role in an uncertain environment. The presence of uncertainty requires an agent to bear the burden of incorrect decisions. The entrepreneur is called upon to forecast consumers' wants and be responsible for the results of his decisions. Knight's distribution theory simply gives the entrepreneur a residual, pure profit for his function. Pure profit is not based on typical productivity considerations; it is an unimputable return. It is necessary, however, as the incentive which induces the entrepreneur to make decisions and take chances.

To summarize, the three theorists discussed in this section made uncertainty the key element in their entrepreneurial theories. Cantillon has the entrepreneur buying at a certain price and selling at an unknown price. Hawley's entrepreneur takes responsibility by virtue of his ownership rights. The Knightian entrepreneur makes decisions for which he is ultimately responsible. The common characteristic in these fundamental roles is the bearing of uncertainty. Without the entrepreneur, production could not take place in an uncertain environment. Uncertainty paralyzes the productive process. The entrepreneur counters uncertainty, allowing production and distribution to operate. The functional role is very much that of a buffer, shielding the economy from uncertainty.

It is interesting to note that none of these authors who emphasized uncertainty cast the entrepreneur as a fourth productive factor (Hawley, in particular, was adamant on this point). For Cantillon, the entrepreneur's uncertainty-bearing allows exchange to occur; he is a necessary distributive agent. The uncertainty borne by Hawley's entrepreneur provides the motivational or purposive drive behind production; he is a necessary causal force. Knight's entrepreneur is an agent willing to be responsible for a decision that requires judgment. Because of the presence of uncertainty, the price system is no longer the perfect sounding board of consumers' wants. The Knightian entrepreneur assumes the role of chooser of products and methods; he is a necessary decision-making agent.

Profit is the reward for exercising the entrepreneurial function. In an uncertain environment, expected and realized results are bound to diverge; perfect coordination is an impossibility. At the junction of an imperfect fit is a profit or loss. The entrepreneur is responsible for these discrepancies, realizing gains and bearing losses. Importantly, it is the anticipation of profit, not its magnitude, that provides the needed incentive.

In an uncertain environment, the entrepreneur comes to the fore by making production, exchange, and distribution possible. The entrepreneur, in a world characterized by uncertainty, is the fundamental agent in the economic system.

Conclusion

This chapter provides a review of the main entrepreneurial roles in the history of economic thought. By focusing on particular entrepreneurial functions, we can categorize diverse theories of entrepreneurship by functional role. Fundamentally, there are four entrepreneurial functions: coordination, arbitrage, innovation, and uncertainty-bearing.

Jean-Baptiste Say presented the role of entrepreneur as coordinator. As the crucial factor in human industry, the entrepreneur hired and combined the other productive agents. The entrepreneur plays a critical role as an actual factor of production. Israel Kirzner represents the Austrian view of the entrepreneur as arbitrageur. The entrepreneur, charged by 'human action', drives the market process. His role is that of an equilibrating mechanism, noticing profit opportunities and moving to fill the gap. Joseph Schumpeter developed a theory of economic development and business cycles based on the entrepreneur as innovator. By breaking new ground, creating 'new combinations', the entrepreneur shattered the circular flow and forced progress. Finally, the entrepreneur as uncertainty-bearer was seen by several theorists as the agent who conquered uncertainty, allowing the productive process to continue. Richard Cantillon's entrepreneur as speculator undertook the risk of an uncertain selling price, allowing exchange to take place. Frederick Hawley's entrepreneur as responsible owner bore the risks of ownership, giving him the power to direct production. Frank Knight's entrepreneur as responsible decision-maker was accountable for the results of a decision liable to error, allowing such decisions to be made.

A tome could be written on the connections and contradictions between these theories. Superficial observation shows the link between Say's entrepreneur in 'commercial industry' and Cantillon's speculator. And what of the role of uncertainty? Hawley focuses on ownership and Knight on decision-making, but the underlying key element, uncertainty, is the same. Cantillon's speculator is clearly Kirzner's arbitrageur in an uncertain environment. On the other hand, Kirzner's entrepreneur equilibrates, while Schumpeter's, seemingly, does the exact opposite. Is a Schumpeterian imitator a Kirznerian entrepreneur? Say's entrepreneur is a fourth factor of production; Hawley rails against such a definition, arguing that the entrepreneur is a motivational force and should never be cast as another factor of production.

These issues are even more interesting when we consider the development of these theories. For example, Schumpeter certainly read Say's *Treatise*. The impact on the Schumpeterian theory is clear: it is only a small jump from entrepreneur as combiner to entrepreneur as creator of new combinations.

For us, however, the most important point lies in the fundamental characteristic shared by all entrepreneurial theories – the central position granted to the entrepreneurial function. For all of these theorists, for a wide variety of reasons, the disappearance of the entrepreneur would bring the market system to a halt. For some, the prime motivational or causal element in production would be lost. Others would have the distributive process unable to function. Still others would see no possible way for growth and development to take place.

This chapter categorizes the various functional roles the entrepreneur has played in the history of economic thought. But, more importantly, it attempts to convey the fundamental and indispensable nature of these roles. From a wide variety of viewpoints, spanning place and time, the entrepreneur has been investigated as the key to our understanding of the market system.

Notes

1 The little research into the history of entrepreneurship that has been done proceeds along these lines. See, for example, J. A. Schumpeter, *History of Economic Analysis*, (London: George Allen & Unwin, 1954) and R. Hebert and A. Link, *The Entrepreneur: Mainstream Views and Radical Critiques*, (New York: Praeger, 1982).

2 The *Traite d'économie politique* first appeared in 1803; four editions, heavily revised, followed. The fourth edition (1819) was translated into English by C. R. Prinsep in 1821.

3 Hebert and Link, *The Entrepreneur*, p. 40.

4 Schumpeter, *History of Economic Analysis*, p. 645.

5 G. Koolman, 'Say's conception of the role of the entrepreneur', *Economica*, New Series 38 (1971); 282–86.

6 Jean-Baptiste Say, *A Catechism in Political Economy*, trans. by John Richter (New York: Augustus M. Kelley, 1967; originally published 1821), p. 26.

7 Jean-Baptiste Say, *A Treatise on Political Economy*, 4th edn, trans. by C. R. Prinsep (Philadelphia: John Grigg, 1830; originally published 1803), p. 14.

8 Say, *Catechism*, pp. 8–10.

9 Say, *Treatise*, p. 20.

10 Say, *Treatise*, p. 21.

11 Say, *Treatise*, p. 268.

12 Say, *Treatise*, p. 279.

13 Say, *Treatise*, p. 23.

14 Say, *Treatise*, p. 285.

15 Say, *Treatise*, p. 22.

16 Say, *Treatise*, p. 285.

17 Say, *Treatise*, p. 286.

18 Say, *Treatise*, p. 287.

19 Say, *Treatise*, p. 278.

20 Say, *Treatise*, p. 285.

21 Say, *Treatise*, p. 285.

22 Say, *Treatise*, p. 285.

23 Say, *Treatise*, p. 286.

24 Say, *Catechism*, pp. 28–9.

25 Koolman, 'Say's conception of the role of the entrepreneur', p. 276.

26 See Israel M. Kirzner (ed.), *Method, Process and Austrian Economics* (Lexington, Mass.: Lexington Books, 1982), pp. 139–59 for Kirzner's view of the relevant issues; Herbert and Link, *The Entrepreneur*, pp. 95–100 for the critics' side.

27 See, for example, Ludwig Lachmann, *Capital, Expectations, and the Market Process*, Walter E. Grinder ed. (Kansas City: Sheed Andrews and McMeel, 1977), especially, 'Some notes on economic thought, 1933–1953', p. 133–48.

28 Israel M. Kirzner, *Competition and Entrepreneurship* (Chicago: University of Chicago Press, 1973), p. 5.

29 This is the Walrasian version of the equilibrating process. Marshallian equilibration is different in that quantity is the adjusting variable, but the analysis is essentially the same.

30 Kirzner, *Competition and Entrepreneurship*, p. 6.

31 Kirzner, *Competition and Entrepreneurship*, p. 10.

32 Lionel Robbins, *An Essay on the Nature of Significance of Economic Science* (London: Macmillan, 1962; originally published 1932), p. 1–23.

33 Israel M. Kirzner, *Perception, Opportunity and Profit* (Chicago: University of Chicago Press, 1979), p. 7.

34 Kirzner, *Perception*, p. 12.

35 Kirzner, *Competition and Entrepreneurship*, p. 16.

36 Kirzner, *Competition and Entrepreneurship*, p. 41.

37 Kirzner, *Perception*, pp. 8–9.

38 Kirzner, *Competition and Entrepreneurship*, p. 48.

39 Kirzner, *Competition and Entrepreneurship*, p. 48.

40 Israel M. Kirzner, 'The primacy of entrepreneurial discovery,' in *The Prime Mover of Progress: The Entrepreneur in Capitalism and Socialism* (London: Institute of Economic Affairs, 1980), p. 10.

41 Kirzner, *Competition and Entrepreneurship*, p. 51.

42 Kirzner, *Perception*, p. 11.

43 Erich Schneider, *Joseph A. Schumpeter*, trans. by W. E. Kuhn, (Lincoln, Neb.: Bureau of Business Research, 1975; originally published 1970), p. 17.

44 Joseph A. Schumpeter, *The Theory of Economic Development* (Cambridge, Mass.: Harvard University Press, 1934; originally published 1911), p. 16.

45 Schumpeter, *Economic Development*, p. 16.

46 Schumpeter, *Economic Development*, p. 17 (footnote omitted).

47 Schumpeter, *Economic Development*, p. 20.

48 Schumpeter, *Economic Development*, p. 20.

49 Schumpeter, *Economic Development*, p. 21.

50 Schumpeter, *Economic Development*, p. 43.

51 Schumpeter, *Economic Development*, p. 44.

52 Schumpeter, *Economic Development*, p. 45.

53 Schumpeter, *Economic Development*, p. 64.

54 Schumpeter, *Economic Development*, p. 66.

55 Schneider, *Joseph A. Schumpeter*, p. 15.

56 Schumpeter, *Economic Development*, p. 106.
57 Schumpeter, *Economic Development*, p. 77.
58 Schumpeter, *Economic Development*, p. 85.
59 Schumpeter, *Economic Development*, p. 86.
60 Schumpeter, *Economic Development*, p. 86.
61 Niccolo Machiavelli, *The Prince* (New York: The New American Library, 1980; originally published 1537), pp. 49–50.
62 Schumpeter, *Economic Development*, p. 93.
63 Schumpeter, *Economic Development*, p. 75.
64 It is true, however, that Schumpeter later argues that class considerations are important. See Joseph A. Schumpeter, *Capitalism, Socialism and Democracy* (New York: Harper and Brothers Publishers, 1942).
65 Schumpeter, *Economic Development*, p. 128.
66 Joseph A. Schumpeter, *Business Cycles*, vol. 1 (New York: McGraw Hill, 1939), p. 105 (footnote omitted).
67 Schumpeter, *Business Cycles*, p. 132.
68 Schumpeter, *Economic Development*, p. 152.
69 Schumpeter, *Economic Development*, p. 153.
70 Richard Cantillon, *Essai sur la Nature du Commerce en General*, ed. and trans. by Henry Higgs (London: Macmillan and Co. Ltd., 1931; originally published 1730–4), p. 51.
71 Cantillon, *Essai*, p. 49.
72 Cantillon, *Essai*, p. 49.
73 Cantillon, *Essai*, p. 55.
74 Cantillon, *Essai*, p. 55.
75 Frederick B. Hawley, *Enterprise and the Productive Process* (New York: G. P. Putnam's Sons, 1907), p. 11.
76 Hawley, *Enterprise*, p. 307.
77 Hawley, *Enterprise*, p. 94.
78 Hawley, *Enterprise*, p. 307.
79 Hawley, *Enterprise*, pp. 331–2.
80 Hawley, *Enterprise*, p. 126.
81 Hawley, *Enterprise*, pp. 306–7.
82 Hawley, *Enterprise*, p. 307.
83 Hawley, *Enterprise*, p. 13.
84 Frank H. Knight, *Risk, Uncertainty and Profit* (New York: Houghton Mifflin Company, 1921). p. 197.
85 Knight, *Risk, Uncertainty and Profit*, p. 268.
86 Knight, *Risk, Uncertainty and Profit*, p. 268.
87 Knight, *Risk, Uncertainty and Profit*, p. 297.
88 Knight, *Risk, Uncertainty and Profit*, p. 308.

Chapter two

The disappearance of the entrepreneur from microeconomic theory – a history

Introduction

In this chapter, we review entrepreneurial investigations through-out the history of economic thought. We find that economic theory is, initially, rich in entrepreneurial debate. Economists discuss the merits and drawbacks of entrepreneurship in the various roles outlined in the previous chapter. Even after marginalism and equilibrium concepts are widely accepted, microeconomists continue to discuss the entrepreneur. In the late 1930s, however, the entrepreneur disappears from the mainstream; he is no longer a fundamental element in the standard microeconomic explanatory scheme. In the *History of Economic Analysis*, Schumpeter briefly mentions the decline of the entrepreneur in conventional econ-omic thought. He notes that the discussion of enterprise reached a peak, producing 'some of its best performances in the 1920s, and finally petered out so far as its theoretical component is concerned'.[1] But the analysis of entrepreneurial issues did far more than just 'peter out'; it actually regressed.

Our goal, in this chapter, is to trace this changing view of entrepreneurship from a much discussed and debated issue to a totally neglected one; we must explicitly trace the rise and fall of the entrepreneur in the history of microeconomic thought. We can then begin to answer the fundamental question: Why did the entrepreneur disappear?

In analyzing different entrepreneurial theories, we will apply the framework of organization developed in the second chapter. Most of the ideas on entrepreneurship are simply a combination of the basic entrepreneurial roles (coordination, arbitrage, inno-vation, and uncertainty-bearing). And much of the disagreement found in the literature has its root causes in differing emphases of the basic entrepreneurial roles.

Once again, the objective is not a ranking of theories or

47

determination of priority, but a review of ideas on entrepreneurship. There is no measure of correctness for a particular view of entrepreneurship – the key is that it is being discussed at all. We will find that consideration of entrepreneurship is quite suddenly removed from the research agenda of mainstream economic theory.

The analysis of entrepreneurial issues in economic thought proceeds by dividing the history of microtheory into three main periods. Early neoclassical thought contains the beginnings of microeconomic theory and continues to the eve of the First World War. Mature neoclassical thought includes the period from 1914 to roughly the early 1930s, just before the complete development of the modern theory of the firm. Finally, the modern microeconomic era is the golden age of microeconomics; the Hicks-Samuelson-Allen *et al.* exposition of the modern theory of the firm.

Our objective is not to compile a comprehensive review of entrepreneurial research during these three periods, but simply to trace the development and use of the entrepreneur through the history of microeconomic theory. Therefore, we will adopt our earlier strategy, selecting for review the work of several representative figures in each era.

The early neoclassical era

In this section, we review the entrepreneurial research of early microeconomic theorists – those writing between 1870 and 1914. We find that entrepreneurial considerations played a prominent role in early neoclassical theories of production and distribution.

By 1870, the classical system (the reigning orthodoxy) was greatly weakened; the wages fund doctrine had been totally rejected and general disenchantment with the classical orthodoxy had reached its peak. The early 1870s saw the simultaneous 'discovery' of marginalism by Leon Walras, William Jevons, and Carl Menger. This ushered in the neoclassical era of economics.

For our purposes, we need to determine the effect of the marginal revolution, that is, the rise of microeconomics, on entrepreneurial theories. Although we have seen that Jean-Baptiste Say argued forcefully that the entrepreneur and capitalist be considered as separate entities, most classical economists simply lumped the two together and called the agent a capitalist. This does not mean, however, that the classical economists ignored entrepreneurship; on the contrary, they were much concerned with technological change and explaining the market system. Unfortunately, they mixed the role of entrepreneur with that of the capitalist. But since the capitalist was a key agent in the classical system, the classicals had, by their association of capitalist and entrepreneur, made entrepreneurship – implicitly – a critical element.

Early neoclassical theorists understood the differences between the two functions and consequently divorced entrepreneurship from capital ownership. They then focused on entrepreneurial issues, casting the entrepreneur as arbitrageur, coordinator, innovator, and uncertainty-bearer. There was no general agreement on the entrepreneur's function in the market system, but such a finding, for our purposes, is irrelevant. The key point is that research into entrepreneurship was an integral part of early neoclassical economic thought. In a variety of ways, the entrepreneur was central in the writings of the early neoclassical economists.

In reviewing early neoclassical entrepreneurial thought, we proceed by examining representative works. We begin, quite naturally, with Leon Walras – arguably the father of neoclassical economics. We then focus on the English neoclassicals, examining Francis Edgeworth's and Alfred Marshall's work on entrepreneurship. Finally, we turn our attention to the United States. Having already discussed Frederick Hawley, we review the works of Irving Fisher and John Bates Clark. By examining the works of leading early neoclassical economists, we hope to convey the fundamental role played by the entrepreneur in early neoclassical thought. The taxonomy developed in the previous chapter is used as a means of categorizing the different roles played by the entrepreneur.

Leon Walras

Walras' entrepreneurial theory contains elements of coordination and arbitrage. For Walras, the entrepreneur played an important role as the coordinator of resources.

> In addition, let us designate by the term entrepreneur a fourth person, entirely distinct from those just mentioned [landowner, laborer, and capitalist], whose role it is to lease land from the land-owner, hire personal faculties from the labourer, and borrow capital from the capitalist, in order to combine the three productive services in agriculture, industry, or trade.[2]

One can clearly see the influence of Walras' French predecessor, J. B. Say, in this aspect of the Walrasian entrepreneur. However, Walras warns against 'the error of a certain number of French economists who look upon the entrepreneur as a worker charged with the special task of managing a firm'.[3] For Walras, entrepreneurship is not simply a fourth factor of production because the entrepreneur plays another, equally crucial, role – that of arbitrageur. In this role, the entrepreneur connects markets, dealing simultaneously with consumers on the product markets and productive agents on the input markets.

Turning to the distribution side, Walras argues that the entrepreneur as coordinator and arbitrageur receives a profit for his services. Walras clearly defines profit as an economic profit – any excess of revenue over explicit and implicit costs. Profit is the signal that allocates resources; the entrepreneur is the agent who responds to that signal. The 'desire to avoid losses and to make profits is the mainspring of the entrepreneur's actions in demanding productive services and offering products for sale'.[4] Thus the entrepreneur as arbitrageur drives the market toward equilibrium

It is here that Walras decides to abandon the entrepreneur. Walras' principal goal is the derivation of the fundamental economic laws governing a general equilibrium state; the *Elements* is a study in 'pure economics'. As such, he clearly and correctly argued that

> we may even go so far as to abstract from entrepreneurs and simply consider the productive services as being, in a certain sense, exchanged directly for one another, instead of being exchanged first against products, and then against productive services.[5]

Thus in Walras' general equilibrium system, the entrepreneur as coordinator and arbitrageur was nonexistent, as were profits. This is not to say the entrepreneur received no income; implicit payments constituted his remuneration. Even in general equilibrium the entrepreneur provides land, labor, and capital services to the firm for which he

> ought to charge to business expense and credit to his own account (the corresponding) rent, wages, and interest charges calculated according to the going market prices of productive services. In this way he earns his living without necessarily making any profits or suffering any losses as an entrepreneur.

For his focus on general equilibrium and the resulting removal of the entrepreneur, Walras has been heavily criticized. Schumpeter, one of Walras' greatest admirers, credits him with an 'important though negative'[7] contribution to entrepreneurial theory.[8] But this is unfair: Walras clearly understood the dominant role of the entrepreneur in a 'real world' environment. His focus, however, was on the solution to a hypothetical, general equilibrium system in which the entrepreneur as coordinator and arbitrageur had already fulfilled his function. In a disequilibrium situation the entrepreneur would play a major role, but Walras' goal was the explanation of the workings of a general equilibrium environment. To this end, he simplified tremendously, going so far as to eliminate, for purposes of exposition, the entrepreneur from his explanatory scheme.

Walras' contribution to entrepreneurial issues was not particularly significant. In the 'real world', he cast the entrepreneur as coordinator and arbitrageur, but then neglected to pursue the entrepreneur as a fundamental agent. We have argued, however, that this neglect was a product of the nature of the questions Walras chose to investigate – the workings of a long-run, perfectly competitive general equilibrium. Outside of this special environment, Walras was clearly aware of the special nature of entrepreneurship.

Francis Edgeworth

Francis Edgeworth never presented a fully developed theory of entrepreneurship. His main role was as a participant in the 'zero profit controversy'. On the production side, Edgeworth accepted the conventional view of the entrepreneur as coordinator and arbitrageur:

> The central figure in the productive system is the entrepreneur. Buying the factors of production, the use of land, labor, machinery, and working them up into half-manufactured or finished products, which he sells to other entrepreneurs or consumers, at a price covering his expenses and remunerating his work and waiting.[9]

The orthodox, or marginal productivity, theory of distributive shares, however, was another matter. Edgeworth was never able to understand the Walrasian claim of a profitless entrepreneur in general equilibrium. Edgeworth's disagreement with Walras over this issue becme known as the 'zero profit controversy'. Unlike Walras, Edgeworth argued that there was a permanent stream of income, called profit, accruing to the entrepreneur: 'That level [of profit] may be low. . . . But that it is normally zero neither common sense nor economic theory compels us to believe.'[10]

Edgeworth understood the marginal productivity distribution theory; he simply argued it was inapplicable to the factor entrepreneurship.

> [There is no] reason for regarding the remuneration of the
> entrepreneur as the product of the number of doses (e.g.
> hours worked) and the marginal productivity of a dose. . . .
> It is only with respect to factors of production which are
> articles of exchange that the proposed law of remuneration,
> the 'law of marginal productivity,' is fulfilled in a regime of
> competition.[11]

For Edgeworth, the entrepreneur pays the factors according to
their marginal productivities, and then claims the residual, that is,
profit. There is no particular relationship between 'entrepreneurial
services' and the residual.

Basically, Edgeworth is distinguishing between 'factors of production which are articles of exchange' and factors, namely
entrepreneurship, which are not traded. The entrepreneur performs necessary functions, coordination and arbitrage, but his
work is such that it cannot be rewarded in the same way as other
factor returns because supply and demand curves for entrepreneurship do not exist.

Edgeworth criticizes those who do not consider the special
nature of entrepreneurship. In particular, he ridicules Philip H.
Wicksteed's (a contemporary English economist) claim that all
factors are remunerated according to the 'universal' law of marginal productivity.

> There is a magnificence in this generalization which recalls the
> youth of philosophy. Justice is a perfect cube, said the ancient
> sage; and rational conduct is a homogeneous function, adds
> the modern savant. A theory which points to conclusions so
> paradoxical [zero profit] ought surely to be enunciated with
> caution.[12]

For Edgeworth, the entrepreneur as coordinator (combining factors of production) and as middleman (connecting product and
factor markets) never disappears, even in general equilibrium. He
is rewarded for his productive services by a return called profit,
which also never disappears and is not a function of marginal
productivity. Edgeworth sees the entrepreneur's function as arbitrageur and coordinator in light of his theory of exchange. In
order for exchange to take place, mutually beneficial gains must
be generated. Those who believe the entrepreneur receives no
profit are 'placed under the heavy burden of having to prove the
consumer qua consumer obtains no pleasure'.[13]

To the modern reader, Edgeworth's argument seems indefen-
sible, a product of a severe confusion between partial and general

equilibrium or between theory and reality. This, however, would be an incorrect evaluation of Edgeworth's understanding of economics. The key to Edgeworth's argument lies in his refusal to admit that a market for entrepreneurship exists. This separates the entrepreneur from the other factors – not on the production, but on the distribution side. Edgeworth believed that the entrepreneur was somehow special or different: he wasn't paid according to marginal productivity, but was a residual claimant. And this residual could not possibly be zero for any sustained period of time. Therefore he argued against the simple elimination, *à la* Walras, of the entrepreneur from the explanatory scheme.

It is true that, as we initially pointed out, Edgeworth never developed a theory of entrepreneurship. But as with Walras, there is an understanding of the special nature of the entrepreneurial function. Walras assumed the problem away by focusing on a general equilibrium environment. Edgeworth's strategy was to refuse to treat the entrepreneur's remuneration analogously to other factors. For Edgeworth, a central place for the entrepreneur must always be maintained.

Whether or not Edgeworth's ideas on profit and entrepreneurship are correct is not at issue here. The important point is that a believer of marginalism, a leading neoclassical economist, recognized special characteristics in the entrepreneur and refused to eliminate entrepreneurial considerations from his explanatory scheme.

Alfred Marshall

By reviewing Alfred Marshall's ideas on the role of the entrepreneur in the productive process, we will be examining simultaneously the dominant neoclassical view of entrepreneurship. From the publication of his *Principles* in 1890 until the 1930s, Marshall controlled neoclassical thought; Alfred Marshall was neoclassical orthodoxy.

In general, Marshall's theories can be aptly described as eclectic, drawing various ideas together in an attempt to describe the total picture. His theory of the functional role of the entrepreneur was no different. The Marshallian entrepreneur was, depending on the matter at hand, coordinator, arbitrageur, innovator, and uncertainty-bearer.

Marshall's view of the market system centers on a special class, the undertakers (or entrepreneurs) who drive the productive process. 'They "adventure" or "undertake" its [production's] risks; they bring together the capital and the labour required for the

53

work; they arrange or "engineer" its general plan, and super-intend its minor details.'[14] Marshall never states precisely the entrepreneur's function; instead, he describes throughout the course of his work various entrepreneurial roles. As uncertainty-bearers and coordinators, entrepreneurs 'undertake the chief risks of the business, and control its general direction'.[15]

Entrepreneurs are coordinators not only because they hire and combine resources, but also because they ceaselessly apply the principle of substitution. The alert undertaker constantly tries to minimize cost, 'to obtain better results with a given expenditure, or equal results with a less expenditure'.[16] Thus the entrepreneur as coordinator guarantees that the $MP_i/w_i = MP_j/w_j$ cost-minimizing first-order condition holds.

In his quest for minimizing cost, the entrepreneur constantly tries new techniques and different ideas. Thus the Marshallian entrepreneur is also an innovator: 'The tendency to variation is the chief cause of progress; and the abler are the undertakers in any trade, the greater will this tendency be.'[17]

Marshall did not, however, simply describe entrepreneurial roles; he used the entrepreneur to explain his 'biological theory' of the rise and fall of firms. The entrepreneur was the head of the firm, the ultimate coordinator and uncertainty-bearer. In this role, Marshall argued that the undertaker was the chief cause of the growth and decline of firms. The young undertaker is full of vitality and ambition, resulting in rapid growth. This will continue 'as long as his energy and enterprise, his inventive and organizing power retain their full strength and freshness, and so long as the risks which are inseparable from business do not cause him insuperable losses'.[18] Unlimited growth is checked, however, by a decline in business ability because 'sooner or later age tells on them all . . . the guidance of the business falls into the hands of people with less energy and less creative genius.'[19]

On the production side, Marshall's entrepreneur performs several tasks: directing production, applying the principle of substitution, trying new techniques, and bearing uncertainty. Through these varied functions, the Marshallian undertaker induces progress and is responsible for the rise and decline of firms.

On the distribution side, Marshall tells the now-familiar neo-classical story. The entrepreneur pays the factors according to their respective marginal productivities, keeping the residual – gross profits – for himself. Gross profit contains interest, wages of management, and a premium for risk-bearing.[20] Furthermore, entrepreneurs with exceptional talents will receive additional income as a 'rent of ability', which is often the largest share.[21]

Profits serve the usual incentive function. Any profits in excess of normal will induce entry; losses will lead to exit. 'Normal' profit is defined tautologically as 'a more or less definite rate of profits on the turnover which is regarded as a "fair" or normal rate'.[22]

Marshall's writings on the entrepreneur are a combination of various ideas on entrepreneurship. His partial equilibrium view naturally led to a focus on particular markets and firms. The entrepreneur is a business leader and head of the firm, innovating, coordinating, responding to profit signals, and bearing risk. His return, gross profits, includes payments for risk-bearing, interest on capital given to the firm, and wages of management.

Marshall was an economic theorist with one foot always in the 'real world'. He saw clearly the importance of leadership and management in the business world and emphasized these functions in his theory. It cannot be said that Marshall developed a theory based exclusively on the entrepreneur, but neither, on the other hand, can it be argued that he neglected entrepreneurial consider-ations. A fair appraisal would recognize the key, but not singularly dominant, roles played by the entrepreneur in Marshallian theory. Marshallian theory was neoclassical, orthodox economics for 40 years. During that period, spanning our early and mature eras, the entrepreneur played a key role in the neoclassical explanation of the market system.

Irving Fisher

Irving Fisher's writings on the entrepreneur, like those of all Americans during the early neoclassical period, focus on the pro-blems created by an uncertain environment. For Fisher, the entrepreneur counterbalances the paralyzing effects of randomness.

Fisher characterized the entrepreneur as the agent who claimed the excess of revenues over costs. In an uncertain environment, the residual claimant's income would be unknown before the product was sold and the factors of production were paid. This element of variability in earnings is the only reason labor is subdiv-ided into workers and entrepreneurs. As a result of the presence of uncertainty, 'workmen classify themselves into two groups – wage earners or employees and enterprisers or employers'.[23] Employees 'wish to avoid chance', while employers 'are willing to assume risks'.[24] The employee removes economic uncertainty from his life; he is told what to do and receives a guaranteed payment. The enterpriser, on the other hand, bears uncertainty. One of his chief functions is to make forecasts, to decide what to do based on subjective expectations. The entrepreneur needs no capital, but typically he is a capitalist as well as an undertaker.

The entrepreneur, once he has made his forecast, acts upon it by hiring and combining factors of production. Fisher discusses the special qualities and abilities needed for carrying out this aspect of the entrepreneurial function, including leadership, judgment, and the like.

After payment of guaranteed wages and other input prices, the entrepreneur gains the residual profit. In theory, profits and wages should be roughly equal. However, in reality, profits are often much higher than wages.

> The employers' or enterprisers' profits tend to be high for three reasons: (1) because these persons assume risks and responsibilities which few are able or willing to take; (2) because for that very reason qualities of foresight, courage and exceptional ability, which few possess, are required; and (3) because the work of the enterpriser usually requires, for its success on a large scale, the possession of capital.[25]

The actual magnitude of profits depends on chance and entrepreneurial ability. Though large profits may seem unjust to the layperson, they are a necessary result of the efficient working of the market system. Profits are a reward and a return for accurate forecasting and superior ability. Large profits 'may be said to be a well-deserved reward for the general good their [the enterprisers'] sagacity brings the public'.[26]

For Fisher, the entrepreneur's importance and distinctiveness are due to his role as profit-receiver. Profit is a special income, present because of the surrounding uncertainty. The entrepreneur, by extension, is a special element, shielding others from unwanted randomness. For this indispensable function, Fisher credits the enterpriser-capitalist as the 'leading figure in modern industry'.[27]

John Bates Clark

In Chapter 1 we examined Frederick Hawley's entrepreneur as uncertainty-bearer. Hawley's entrepreneur provided a buffer against uncertainty by bearing risk through product ownership. John B. Clark vehemently opposed this characterization of the entrepreneur. Their debate dominated entrepreneurial investigations in the United States during the early neoclassical era.

Interestingly enough, the modern reader, when comparing Hawley and Clark, is usually struck by their similarities rather than their differences. For Clark, the fundamental essence of the entrepreneurial role lies in the 'acquiring and surrendering of ownership'.[28] Instead of distinguishing between certain and uncertain states, Clark juxtaposes static and dynamic economies. In a static economy, characterized by perfect competition, the entrepreneur disappears.

Clark's entrepreneur is an arbitrageur in a dynamic economy. The essence of entrepreneurship is not superintendence or management, although that is often its most visible manifestation. Similarly, the entrepreneur is usually a capitalist. But if the entrepreneur fills the management and capitalist functions, it merely means he needs management and capital and has chosen to hire himself. The true entrepreneurial role is 'a special coordinating function which is not labor, in the technical sense, and scarcely involves any continuous personal activity at all, but is essential for rendering labor and capital productive'.[29] In a dynamic economy, the entrepreneur hires factors to create a product with a higher value than they were previously producing: '[This] results in placing labor and capital where they can produce more than they have done and more than they could do were it not for the enabling act of the enterpriser which places them on a vantage ground of superiority.'[30]

Clark's entrepreneur is not a factor of production, not an uncertainty-bearer, and not a capitalist. He performs a purely mercantile function, paying for the elements of a product and then selling the product. Here we find the fundamental disagreement between Clark and Hawley. Clark's entrepreneur is not an uncertainty-bearer; risk is borne by the capitalist. The entrepreneur induces further progress by shifting resources towards their most profitable uses. He is an arbitrageur in a dynamic system. The entrepreneur in Clark's dynamic system makes decisions about what to produce, where to sell, for how much, and so on. In this role, not as uncertainty-bearer, he protects the economy from the paralyzing effects of the unknown. For Clark, the entrepreneur owns products, not to bear uncertainty, but to gain the power of direction.

Clark's theory of distribution casts the entrepreneur as the 'universal paymaster'. Factors are rewarded according to marginal productivity, including a wage for management. In a static system, this exactly exhausts the total product. In a dynamic system, however, an additional income accrues to a new agent, the entrepreneur. Profit is a return for 'the function of hiring both capital and labor and getting whatever their joint product is worth above the cost of the elements which enter into it'.[31] Profit is a return for arbitrage and it is claimed by the entrepreneur by virtue of his role as director of resources. Profit bears no particular relation to ability; it is a return for the alertness to a more lucrative use of resources: '[Profit] is always determined residually. It is a remainder and nothing else. . . . It is the only share in distribution that is so determined. Enterpriser's profits and residual income are synonymous terms.'[32]

As usual, profits play their signalling role. Entrepreneurs respond to excess profits – anything over cost – by increasing production. This increases cost and lowers price, squeezing profits, eventually, to zero.

Clark's entrepreneur performs the purely mercantile function of arbitrage in a dynamic system. In this role, the entrepreneur is the moving force behind the economy, responding to profit opportunities by shifting resources. In return, the entrepreneur receives a residual reward, profit – the only income so determined. The differences between Hawley and Clark – an uncertain versus a dynamic environment and, consequently, the entrepreneur as uncertainty-bearer versus arbitrageur – were the focus of much discussion in the United States during the early neoclassical period. No attempt to declare a winner is made here; we simply note the crucial, yet different functions of the entrepreneur in the theories of these two early neoclassical economists.

To conclude this part of our review, during the period from 1870 to 1914, microeconomics was born and grew rapidly. Marginalism and equilibrium concepts were introduced and much discussed. In this environment, research into entrepreneurial issues flourished. Walras understood the importance of the entrepreneur, but neglected him for expository reasons. Edgeworth and Marshall, the leaders of the English neoclassical economists, discussed entrepreneurship and its function in a market economy. None of these early neoclassicals made the entrepreneur the sole element in their economic analysis; importantly, however, they did note the special nature of entrepreneurship.

The Americans, with their overriding concern with uncertainty, focused on the entrepreneur as a key agent. The entrepreneur as uncertainty-bearer was a fundamental actor in the theoretical systems created by Fisher and Hawley. For Clark, the entrepreneur as arbitrageur was an indispensable element in a progressive, dynamic economy.

Neoclassical economics had taken hold and, consequently, microeconomic theory was born; yet research into entrepreneurial issues continued. A variety of alternative theories, especially in the United States, were struggling for dominance, resulting in a lively debate. The merits of the opposing viewpoints are unimportant here; the crucial point is that microeconomic theory was struggling with entrepreneurial issues during this early period. There was no contradiction between entrepreneurship and early neoclassical theory. In fact, the focus on individual behavior seemed destined to focus further attention on the entrepreneur and his role in the market system.

The mature neoclassical era

With the general acceptance of marginalism and equilibrium concepts, neoclassical economics settled down into an era perhaps best termed as Kuhnian 'normal' science. Problems were being cast increasingly in the optimization framework and the Walrasian system was beginning to be understood in the English-speaking world.

During the mature neoclassical era (roughly from the First World War to the early 1930s), entrepreneurial discussion did not die down. In fact, the mature neoclassical era was one in which two of the greatest authors on entrepreneurship – Joseph Schumpeter and Frank Knight – gained broad recognition and acceptance.

As we have already seen, Schumpeter's entrepreneur as innovator was the key to economic development and the regularity of business cycles. The Knightian entrepreneur was the responsible decision-maker in an uncertain environment. Both cast the entrepreneur as a fundamental figure in their explanations of development and the workings of the market system.

During this period, Marshall still reigned supreme in England. His eclectic views on entrepreneurship were generally accepted by the English neoclassical economists. We will not review these rewordings of the Marshallian position; suffice it to say that the entrepreneur as coordinator, uncertainty-bearer, and arbitrageur lived in the minds of mature English neoclassicals. We will review, however, the work of Maurice Dobb, who cast the entrepreneur as an innovator.

In the United States, the first generation of neoclassical economists (F. B. Hawley, J. B. Clark, Frank A. Fetter, Frank W. Tanssig, Herbert J. Davenport, and so on) still dominated the scene and the discussion still centered on uncertainty considerations. Knight's *Risk, Uncertainty and Profit* was a tremendous contribution to the debate. Charles Tuttle, writing in the 1920s, exemplifies the concern with ownership during this time.

Since we have already covered many of the economists during this period (especially Schumpeter and Knight), this section is limited to brief reviews of Dobb's and Tuttle's writings on the entrepreneur. This will help give the reader an accurate picture of research into entrepreneurship during the mature neoclassical era.

Maurice Dobb

Maurice Dobb criticizes all theories that cast the entrepreneur as a passive agent. For Dobb, the market system has none of the 'automatically' efficient properties which most economists take for granted. It is the entrepreneur as an active, purposive element in production that is the driving force behind the capitalist system.

Dobb argues that the modernization of industry has led to a refinement of the entrepreneur's function. In modern capitalism, the entrepreneur need not be a capital owner or manager; instead, the nature of entrepreneurship is something 'essentially active and creative'.[33] In modern industrial society, two different problems must be solved in order to gain the greatest benefits for society. In a static sense, it is true that resources should be allocated to their most productive uses. This adjustment is one of the central problems facing an economy. In addition, there is a crucial dynamic problem: the system must initiate change – the new grouping of resources – in order to increase the yield of human effort. There are three basic types of innovation: innovation in technique; geographical discoveries that change conditions of transport and supply; and innovation in organization.

For Dobb, the entrepreneur is the agent who carries out innovations. The entrepreneur is not a type of laborer; he is a decision-maker willing to try something new based on a subjective interpretation of the surrounding environment. The exercise of the entrepreneurial function is the only way for progress to occur. Development depends on the 'human willingness to face uncertainty and the ability on meagre evidence to make judgments which are approximately correct'.[34]

Thus the entrepreneur is the functional agent responsible for solving the two basic economic problems facing any society – adjustment and innovation. Uncertainty is a fact of life, but the bearing of uncertainty is not essential to the entrepreneurial function. The key lies in decision-making:

> The principle elements of ['the Entrepreneur Function'], as applied to any economic society, will be the capacity for

Adjustment and Innovation; and in the case of the latter the ability to make correct judgments as to the future is, perhaps, the most important.[35]

On the individual firm level, Dobb rejects any notion of a firm that 'runs itself'. All firms need the 'leadership and strategy of a general'.[36] The capitalist undertaker assumes this role.

> Undertakers will be the men who take the ruling decisions in industrial, financial and commercial enterprise. They will perform the composite function of formulating a certain commercial plan and of superintending its execution, of selecting opportunities with an eye to the maximum profit.[37]

Perhaps Dobb's main concern in dealing with the entrepreneur is to reject completely the notion of passive entrepreneurship. On an economy-wide level, the entrepreneur is the active, dynamic agent responsible for change. On the firm level, the entrepreneur actively and aggressively runs the firm and directs production.

On the distribution side, Dobb criticizes the many competing theories of profit. Profit is not a return to a productive service, entrepreneurship. Neither is it an economic rent, a temporary phenomenon due to 'friction' in the system, nor, as Marshall would argue, the sum of all of the above. Dobb's profit theory has profit accruing to entrepreneurs for their special decision-making and innovating role in production. However, the profit so gained is far in excess of the necessary reward. This is due to a variety of barriers to entry that serve to block competition among existing entrepreneurs, including:

- the fact that the ability required is severely limited by nature
- the requisite large initial outlays on education and training
- the considerable capital and influence needed
- the lack of knowledge of available opportunities
- the existing special legal privileges that protect entrenched undertakers
- the existence of large established firms with extensive knowledge and connections[38]

These barriers to entry ensure that competition among existing entrepreneurs 'does not suffice to eliminate profits'.[39] Furthermore, since economic progress constantly generates profits through innovation, even a tendency toward the elimination of profits does not imply that a zero profit state will ever be reached. Thus Dobb's theory of profit is basically a reaction against those who believe in the smooth working of the profit signal and the market system. Dobb grants the entrepreneur a preferred place in production, but argues his profit income as capitalist undertaker is excessive and will not be eroded by competition.

Dobb's entrepreneur as innovator is an attempt to capture what, for Dobb, is the crucial ingredient in entrepreneurship – aggressive, active decision-making. The entrepreneur is the critical agent on both economy-wide and individual firm levels. Distribution also centers around the entrepreneur since he generates and receives the crucial share, profit.

Many readers would seriously question the placement of Maurice Dobb in the category of 'mature neoclassical' economists. Politically, he may have been a Marxist, but *Capitalist Enterprise and Social Progress* is far from a Marxist *economic* treatise. In a footnote, Schumpeter evaluates Dobb's intellectual leanings:

> Maurice Dobb was never impregnated with Marxism;
> allowance must be made for the English environment. But
> his sympathies, intellectual and other, are obviously with Marx
> rather than with Marshall or with the Fabians. Nevertheless,
> he cannot be described as a Marxist so far as *economic analysis
> is concerned*. See his *Capitalist Enterprise and Social Progress*
> (1925).[40]

At any rate, the point is that Dobb's entrepreneur as innovator was perfectly compatible with the ruling mainstream neoclassical analysis. There is no contradiction between the entrepreneur as innovator and mature neoclassical theory. Schumpeter presented his theory of entrepreneurship as innovation in such an environment and so did Maurice Dobb.

Charles Tuttle

In two articles published in 1927,[41] Charles Tuttle set out to 'analyze and define the distinctive function of the entrepreneur'.[42] For Tuttle, the key to a correct understanding of the entrepreneurial role rests on ownership considerations.

On the production side, Tuttle adds a fourth productive factor – organization – to the traditional triad of land, labor and capital. This new factor 'is an essential element in a business'[43] because it provides 'the *opportunities* for the investment of capital, those for the employment of labor, as well as those for the use of land in productive enterprise'.[44]

Once organization is defined, the entrepreneur's function is easily understood. The entrepreneur simply owns the factor organization, just as, for example, the landowner owns the factor land.

As owner of organization, the entrepreneur provides the place where land, labor, and capital meet to produce output.

In order to have a part in the productive process at all, these factors must find their respective places in the organized business unit. The opportunities that await them place them in efficient relationship to each other, and for that reason may very properly be called *opportunities of organization*.[45]

Tuttle clearly distinguishes coordination from organization. The entrepreneur is not a coordinator; he is often cast in such a role because he usually hires himself for that function, but he could just as easily hire someone else. Furthermore, while it is theoretically possible for the entrepreneur to exist solely in his role as entrepreneur, in the real world, 'the function is found always in "personal union" with at least one of the other functions'.[46]

The pure entrepreneur becomes a key element in Tuttle's scheme solely by virtue of his ownership rights. It is 'the element of ownership of the productive opportunities for the other factors [that] gives the function of the entrepreneur its strategic position of dominance in the business as a going concern. It is the *seat of authority in the business unit*'[47] The entrepreneur as owner of organization owns the business unit. In this capacity, he is responsible for any risks associated with production. The entrepreneur is under 'obligation to satisfy all claims upon their [the products'] value, possessed by other participants in its production'.[48] Without the assumption of such a role, production could not continue.

Tuttle briefly discusses the qualities needed for the entrepreneur to carry out his role as responsible owner, including possession of capital (owned or borrowed), a reputation for 'judicious and successful organization', and skill and knowledge.[49]

On the distribution side, Tuttle notes the confused state of profit theory and introduces his views on the subject. He argues that profit is simply a return to ownership. The hired factors are paid by the salaried manager and any residual, the profit, is taken by the entrepreneur by virtue of his ownership of the factor organization and the resulting product. By assuming the function of ownership, and only by this means, the entrepreneur 'becomes entitled to draw from the product of socialized industry an income specifically called profit'.[50] Although very clear on the profit recipient, Tuttle, unfortunately, never explains what determines the magnitude of profits.

Charles Tuttle attempted to plug a perceived hole in orthodox theory by applying a strict definition of entrepreneurship. Tuttle was worried that neoclassical production theory had no meeting place under which factors congregated to produce outputs. His remedy for this problem was straightforward: he created a fourth productive factor, organization, to fill this role. He defined the entrepreneur in a 'strictly scientific way' as the owner of this fourth factor.[51] From his vantage point as responsible owner, the entrepreneur can 'dictate the policy of the organization'.[52] The return to this function is defined as profit, but the determination of its magnitude is left unclear.

Tuttle's entrepreneur as a responsible owner can perhaps best be viewed as an attempt to explain the inner workings of the firm. The emphasis is on organization and the owner of the organization, the entrepreneur. Although far from a comprehensive theory of entrepreneurship, we can see that the entrepreneur plays an active role in Tuttle's analysis.

To summarize, during the period between the First World War and the development of the modern theory of the firm, here called the mature neoclassical period, the entrepreneur was a crucial agent in microeconomic theory. Marshallian economics dominated neoclassical thought and Marshall clearly recognized the importance of the entrepreneur. During this time, Schumpeter and Knight developed their theories of development and change. They accepted the fundamental tenets of standard microtheory – marginalism (marginal utility and productivity) and equilibrium – yet found a central place for the entrepreneur in their views of the working of the market system.

In this section, we reviewed the work of Maurice Dobb and Charles Tuttle as further examples of research dealing with entrepreneurship during the mature neoclassical era. Dobb cast the entrepreneur as an innovating agent; Tuttle's entrepreneur is a responsible owner. For both, the entrepreneur is an important agent in the productive and distributive processes.

Clearly, neoclassical theory had become orthodox economic theory during this time. The crucial point is that the entrepreneur remained a central figure, a key agent in the orthodox neoclassical explanation of the market system. However, microeconomics was now nearing the third phase of its development and a radical change was about to take place.

The era of modern microeconomic theory

During the modern microeconomic period, roughly beginning in the early 1930s and continuing to the present, the entrepreneur – in any meaningful sense of the term – disappeared from microeconomic theory. By 'disappeared', I mean that entrepreneurial

considerations no longer played a fundamental role in the orthodox theoretical explanation of the market system. Discussion of
entrepreneurship as coordination, arbitrage, innovation, or
uncertainty-bearing was simply absent from the explanatory
scheme.

The word 'entrepreneur' was sometimes used, but it lost any
special meaning. Specifically, the entrepreneur's special qualities,
which had previously guaranteed a dominant role for entrepreneurship, were now ignored. The entrepreneur was simply another
element in a very long line of productive inputs. Certainly there
was nothing particularly special or different that separated the
factors of production. Each was needed and equally important;
each performed a specific task, and each was hired and paid a
wage determined by supply and demand.

Thus research into entrepreneurship per se was simply nonexistent. It is very difficult to give the reader a sense of the sudden
neglect of entrepreneurial issues from mainstream microeconomic
thought. There were virtually no articles dealing with entrepreneurship written by leading modern microeconomic theorists. In
1934, Nicholas Kaldor, seeking to show a long-run inconsistency
in the theory of cost, discussed the entrepreneur as coordinator.[53]
Three years later, Ronald Coase equated the entrepreneur with
the firm and argued that lower transaction costs were the firm's
reason for existence.[54] Both of these articles were largely ignored.

Subsequent expositions of standard economic analyses of the
market system made no use of past entrepreneurial functional
definitions. The fruitful theories of innovation, uncertainty-
bearing, coordination, and arbitrage were downplayed or totally
neglected. In this sense, the entrepreneur had disappeared from
microeconomic theory.

The point of this section is short and sweet: there is nothing to
review during the modern microeconomic era because little work
was done dealing with entrepreneurship. Schumpeter was right:
the discussion of enterprise reached a peak, producing 'some of
its best performances in the 1920s, and finally petered out so far
as its theoretical component is concerned'.[55] But, of course, that
leaves us with the question of why this happened.

Conclusion

In this chapter, we have traced research into entrepreneurial considerations throughout microeconomic theory. Initially much discussed, the entrepreneur maintained a high visibility during the
mature neoclassical era, but then was rapidly exorcised in the

modern microeconomic period. The early and mature neoclassical economists ran the full gamut of entrepreneurial theories. In the early period, Walras noted the importance of the entrepreneur as a coordinator and arbitrageur, but eliminated him for purposes of exposition. Edgeworth sparked heated debate by his refusal to admit that a 'zero profit' equilibrium existed. Marshall, the very definition of eclectic, cast the entrepreneur as coordinator, arbitrageur, innovator, and uncertainty-bearer. Finally, the Americans, much concerned with uncertainty, had the entrepreneur conquer uncertainty in a variety of ways.

The mature neoclassical period witnessed the development of two great entrepreneurial theories: Schumpeter's entrepreneur as innovator and the Knightian uncertainty-bearing entrepreneur. In addition, Dobb and Tuttle discussed the entrepreneur as innovator and responsible owner, respectively.

In the modern microeconomic period, the situation changed dramatically: economics witnessed the fall of the entrepreneur from a position of importance. The entrepreneur was not only removed from the focal point of the analysis, he was completely neglected. It is in this sense that it can be said that the entrepreneur disappeared.

Orthodox microeconomic theory had made entrepreneurial considerations an important part of the explanation of the market system for over a half century. Yet in the 1930s this radically changed; the entrepreneur was no longer a central part of the theory. How and why did this happen? Why did entrepreneurship, which had played various fundamental roles over several decades of microeconomic thought and had been discussed before Adam Smith, suddenly disappear?

Notes

1 Joseph A. Schumpeter, *History of Economic Analysis*, Elizabeth B. Schumpeter (ed.) (New York: Oxford University Press, 1954), p. 894.
2 Leon Walras, *Elements of Pure Economics*, trans. by William Jaffe (Homewood, Ill.: Richard D. Irwin, 1954; originally published 1870), p. 222.
3 Walras, *Elements*, p. 222.
4 Walras, *Elements*, p. 225.
5 Walras, *Elements*, p. 225.
6 Walras, *Elements*, p. 276.
7 Schumpeter, *History of Economic Analysis*, p. 893.
8 See also Mark Obrinsky, *Profit Theory and Capitalism* (Philadelphia: University of Pennsylvania Press, 1983), pp. 40–4; and Robert

Hebert and Albert Link, *The Entrepreneur: Mainstream Views and Radical Critiques* (New York: Praeger, 1982), p. 63, for further discussion of this charge.

9 Francis Y. Edgeworth, *Papers Relating to Political Economy*, vol. 2 (London: Macmillan and Co. Ltd., 1925), p. 378.

10 Edgeworth, *Papers*, vol. 2, p. 469.

11 Edgeworth, *Papers*, vol. 1, p. 28.

12 Edgeworth, *Papers*, vol. 1, p. 31.

13 Edgeworth, *Papers*, vol. 2, p. 469.

14 Alfred Marshall, *Principles of Economics*, 9th edn, with annotations by C. W. Guillebaud (New York: Macmillan Co., 1961; originally published 1890), p. 293.

15 Marshall, *Principles*, p. 293.

16 Marshall, *Principles*, p. 355.

17 Marshall, *Principles*, p. 355.

18 Marshall, *Principles*, p. 315.

19 Marshall, *Principles*, p. 316.

20 Marshall, *Principles*, p. 586.

21 Marshall, *Principles*, p. 624.

22 Marshall, *Principles*, p. 617.

23 Irving Fisher, *Elementary Principles of Economics* (New York: Macmillan Co., 1920; originally published 1910), p. 455.

24 Fisher, *Principles*, p. 455.

25 Fisher, *Principles*, p. 457.

26 Fisher, *Principles*, p. 459.

27 Fisher, *Principles*, p. 460.

28 John B. Clark and F. H. Giddings, *The Modern Distributive Process* (Boston: Ginn & Co., 1888), p. 38.

29 J. B. Clark, *Essentials of Economic Theory* (New York: Macmillan Co., 1922), p. 83.

30 Clark, *Essentials*, p. 124.

31 Clark, *Essentials*, p. 85.

32 Clark, *Essentials*, p. 154.

33 Maurice Dobb, *Capitalist Enterprise and Social Progress*, 2nd edn (London: George Rantledge & Sons Ltd., 1926; originally published 1925), p. 19.

34 Dobb, *Capitalist Enterprise*, p. 36.

35 Dobb, *Capitalist Enterprise*, p. 38.

36 Dobb, *Capitalist Enterprise*, p. 53.

37 Dobb, *Capitalist Enterprise*, p. 54.

38 Dobb, *Capitalist Enterprise*, pp. 78–83.

39 Dobb, *Capitalist Enterprise*, p. 85.

40 Schumpeter, *History of Economic Analysis*, p. 884 (emphasis added).

41 Charles Tuttle, 'The function of the entrepreneur', *American Economic Review* 17 (March 1927): 13–25; and Charles Tuttle, 'The entrepreneur in economic literature', *Journal of Political Economy* 35 (August 1927): 501–21.

42 Tuttle, 'The function of the entrepreneur', p. 13.
43 Tuttle, 'The function of the entrepreneur', p. 16.
44 Tuttle, 'The function of the entrepreneur', p. 19 (emphasis added).
45 Tuttle, 'The function of the entrepreneur', p. 19.
46 Tuttle, 'The function of the entrepreneur', p. 22.
47 Tuttle, 'The function of the entrepreneur', p. 20 (emphasis added).
48 Tuttle, 'The function of the entrepreneur', p. 20.
49 Tuttle, 'The function of the entrepreneur', p. 22.
50 Tuttle, 'The function of the entrepreneur', P. 24.
51 Tuttle, 'The function of the entrepreneur', p. 23.
52 Tuttle, 'The function of the entrepreneur', p. 24.
53 Nicholas Kaldor, 'The equilibrium of the firm', *Economic Journal* 44 (March 1934): 60–76.
54 Ronald H. Coase, 'The nature of the firm', *Economica*, New Series 4 (1937): 386–405.
55 Schumpeter, *History of Economic Analysis*, p. 894.

Chapter three

An explanation for the disappearance of the entrepreneur – the description

Introduction

Thus far we have seen the entrepreneur perform four fundamental functions in the history of economics – coordination, arbitrage, innovation, and uncertainty-bearing (Chapter 1). The point that must be stressed is the many different ways the entrepreneur has been used to understand and explain how the market system functions. We have also reviewed entrepreneurial considerations in the history of microeconomic theory by tracing the disappearance of the entrepreneur from standard microeconomics (Chapter 2). We found that it was only during the third stage of the development of microeconomics that the entrepreneur disappeared from the research agenda.

If the entrepreneur has played a variety of crucial roles throughout the history of economic thought, including the early and mature microeconomic eras, then the natural and obvious question is: Why did the entrepreneur disappear from microeconomic theory? An attempt to answer this question thoroughly forms the remainder of this work. All subsequent discussions are geared toward explaining why the entrepreneur disappeared.

An initial obstacle is the definition of 'explanation'. The answer to a 'why?' question directly depends on the level of analysis chosen. For example, to an eyewitness of a murder, explanation consists of a simple retelling of his observations: death was 'caused' by the firing of a gun. A different kind of explanation is the actual process by which an event occurred. Thus to the coroner, the cause of death lies in a complicated medical description. Finally, an explanation can focus on the motivating forces that led to the shooting. For the police detective, an explanation is found when the story behind the shooting – the events that led to the shooting itself – is determined.

We will systematically respond to our question of why the entrepreneur disappeared on these three levels. On the first level of explanation, the description, the answer is simply that the development of the modern theory of the firm led to the demise of the entrepreneur. This is the eyewitness account of the disappearance of the entrepreneur. The second level of explanation, the 'medical cause of death', finds the theoretical assumptions inherent in the modern theory of the firm as the key to the demise of the entrepreneur. Finally, the need to maintain internal consistency within the theoretical structure is found to be the motivating force behind the disappearance of the entrepreneur from microeconomic theory. This is the third and most fundamental level of explanation.

Our three levels of explanation make extensive use of the modern theory of the firm, by which we mean nothing more than present-day, orthodox production and cost theory. This is the view of a firm as a place where inputs are transformed into output and optimization theory is used to determine the optimal values of the endogenous variables. The firm faces three such optimization problems: (1) the isoquant side finds the least expensive mix of inputs that produce a given level of output; (2) the output side problem is to choose the output level that maximizes profits; and (3) the factor market analysis maximizes profits by finding the optimal levels of input use. Importantly, full understanding of the theory of the firm is not reached until the three alternative optimization problems are seen to be three facets of the same problem. The remarkable consistency and interrelatedness of these three ways to view the firm is the hallmark of the modern day theory of the firm. Expositions of the theory of the firm (also known as the Hicks-Allen or Hicks-Samuelson theory of production) can be found in any textbook of economic principles, of price theory, or microeconomics.[1]

In this chapter, we begin our explanation of the disappearance of the entrepreneur from microeconomic theory with a claim that the rise of the modern theory of the firm led to the decline of entrepreneurial considerations during the modern microeconomic era. This chapter is dedicated to providing historical evidence for this statement. Importantly, at this first level of analysis, the goal is simply to determine the reason, as a plain fact, for the disappearance of the entrepreneur. Actual causes and motivations will be discussed in subsequent chapters.

Our claim is composed of two parts: the disappearance of the entrepreneur and the development of the modern theory of the firm. Having already discussed the former (Chapter 2), the next section presents a general review of the history of the modern theory of the firm. A correlation of these two histories is then presented, the results being the historical evidence for our first level of explanation.

A general history of the modern theory of the firm

This section is designed to show the development of the modern theory of the firm. The main goal is to show the systematic movement of the profession as a whole toward the unified theory of production, cost, and distribution that is now known as the modern theory of the firm.

This section, however, is by no means meant to be a comprehensive history of microeconomic theory. Our objective is much less ambitious; we simply want a rough outline, a general history of the theory of the firm.

Unfortunately, the history of microeconomic production theory has never been explicitly laid out. In general, reference is made – if at all – to Hicks and Allen[2] or Hicks and Samuelson as the founders of the modern (mathematical) theory of the firm. But this is beginning at the end; neoclassicals must and did have a theory of the firm before the 1930s. The work of John R. Hicks, Paul Samuelson, and R. G. D. Allen (among others) represented the culmination of years of development. It is this history of development toward the modern theory of the firm that we wish to capture.

Furthermore, the development of the modern theory of the firm is seen from a present perspective, that is, the modern theory of the firm is the benchmark from which we gauge understanding. The history is, essentially, the process of integrating the three facets of the theory (isoquant, output, and factor market) into a cohesive whole. Once this was achieved, the modern theory of the firm was born and has remained basically unchanged.

In this section, we will follow the chronological order of development, tracing the evolution of the factor market, output, and isoquant characterizations. The focus then shifts to synthesis. At this point, an aside discussing the relationship between general and firm equilibrium is necessary. We then analyze the first attempts at merger ('Precursors'), turning finally to the work of those who fully understood the entire system.

As a final note, the reader should not be disconcerted by our failure to mention Leon Walras in the first three sections. Evidence of his brilliant originality and his 'crabbed and obscure' exposition[3] is found in Walras' work on general equilibrium theory. While others were working on a particular facet of the firm, Walras was already trying to integrate the pieces. Walras' efforts singlehandedly destroyed any hope for a continuous, cumulative progression of knowledge in the development of the modern theory of the firm – he was years ahead of his time. His work is analyzed in detail in the sixth section ('The entire system integrated – precursors').

The factor market side – historical development

The historical development of the factor market side (that is, the choice of the profit-maximizing levels of factor use) is slightly confusing because of the early discovery of the law of diminishing returns. From a macroeconomic distribution theory perspective, the classicals (specifically, West, Torrens, Malthus, and Ricardo) used the diminishing returns concept in their analysis of distribution and population. This, however, is a different issue from the factor market side optimization problem. From our perspective, we must look for an understanding of marginal analysis on the factor market side in terms of maximizing net receipts.

The essential element in any maximization problem is that marginal gain must equal marginal cost. For the factor market characterization, we must look for an understanding that inputs should be hired until the marginal revenue product is no longer greater than the marginal factor cost as a sign that the factor market problem is being discussed.

The first to understand and explain the marginal criterion from the factor market side was Johann H. von Thunen. In 1826, he perfectly described the factor market side in his neglected and, later, much criticized *The Isolated State*. Thunen's exposition, completely verbal, is so well put that no apology is necessary for quoting it at length:

> In farming we have many ways of raising not only the immediate but the permanent output of a plot of land; by greater thoroughness of tillage and of harvesting, by bringing in manure, gypsum, bonedust, guano, marl, and mould, or by adding some variety of soil that is lacking in the plot. When such improvements are bought at a cost higher than the value of the additional product they achieve, they not only ruin the farmer who undertakes them, but reduce the total national wealth. For the maximum net product must be the farmer's target, not the maximum gross product. If we ask: How thorough should the farmer be in cultivation and soil improvement? the answer is this: (1) Thoroughness of labour,

in gathering potatoes for example, must not go beyond the point where the last amount of labour spent on the task is still repaid by the higher output achieved. (2) Similarly, soil may only be improved to the point – but not beyond – where the interest on the cost of buying or producing the required manure is still balanced by the higher yield obtained thereby.

A higher yield is always bought at an outlay of capital and labour; there must therefore be a point where the value of the extra yield equals the value of the extra capital and labour spent on it. This is the point which represents the maximum net product.[4]

Verbal analyses of this kind became commonplace, but it was not until Philip Wicksteed's *Essay on the Co-ordination of the Laws of Distribution* (1894) that the graphical and mathematical exposition began to take form. Wicksteed explicitly considered a production function, $P = F(A,B,C, . . .)$, where P is the product and A, B, C, . . . are the inputs.

Then the (marginal) significance of each factor is determined by the effect upon the product of a small increment of that factor, all the others remaining constant. It is suggested that the ratio of participation in the product on which any factor, K, can insist (by the threat of withdrawal), will be dP/dK per unit, and its total share will be $(dP/dK)K$.[5]

But Wicksteed's overriding concern was on distribution in the sense of factor share given that a certain amount of the factor is used. He showed graphically that factor A would receive its marginal revenue product – given that a units of factor A are employed. Wicksteed failed, however, to pose the problem of how much of factor A should be hired in order to maximize profits.

It was Wicksell, as early as 1893 in *Uber Wert, Kapital and Rente*, who showed how to determine the optimal number of workers to hire in order to maximize net receipts. Wicksell found that as long as the landowner (the factor hirer, in this case), by engaging one more laborer, obtains a greater increase in production than the amount by which wages are increased, it will be to his advantage to do so.[6]

Wicksell presented a simple numerical example. He let $Q = 400\sqrt{L}$ represent the production technology, then derived a given product price of 10s and an equilibrium wage of 500s (obtained by constraining the quantity of labor demanded to equal the supply) – and proceeded to solve the problem. The first-order condition is

10s $(200/\sqrt{L})$ = 500s. Solving for the optimum use of labour, it is clear that $L^* = 16$.[7]

Thus Wicksell, writing in the early twentieth century, clearly understood and presented the solution to the factor market side optimization problem. Every input should be hired according to the same decision rule: hire until marginal revenue product equals marginal factor cost.

The next step in the development of the factor market characterization would be the explicit setting up and solving of a factor market maximization problem. This was done, but can be better discussed below when we survey the first attempts to integrate the three facets of the theory of the firm.

The output side – historical development

The historical development of the output side (that is, the choice of the profit-maximizing level of output) is marked by Augustin Cournot's brilliant work in 1838, then little advance until Marshall in 1890. Cournot's *Researches into the Mathematical Principles of the Theory of Wealth* was one of the first works casting economic problems in an optimization framework. Perhaps most famous for his work in duopoly theory, Cournot made the first attempt at describing the firm's output side.

Initially, Cournot analyzed the firm's output optimization problem with the simplifying assumption that no costs were incurred in production. Given the law of demand, $D = F(p)$ (where D is the quantity demanded and p is the price), he showed that the firm should choose that price which satisfies $F(p) + pF'(p) = 0$ in order to maximize total revenue. Cournot even included a discussion of the second-order conditions.

He then complicated the analysis, introducing positive costs of production:

> It will no longer be the function $pF(p)$, or the annual gross receipts, which the producer should strive to carry to its maximum value, but the net receipts, or the function $pF(p) - \emptyset(D)$, in which $\emptyset(D)$ denotes the cost of making a number of liters [the output is mineral spring water] equal to D. . . . Consequently the price to which the producer should bring his article will be determined by the equation
>
> $$D + \frac{dD}{dP} \left[P - \frac{d\left[\emptyset(D)\right]}{dP} \right] = 0.\text{[8]}$$

Cournot must be given credit for being the first to describe the general outline of the output side. He realized that the goal was to make the biggest difference between revenue and cost, a goal easily accomplished by finding the point at which the net revenue function's slope, or first derivative, was zero. Given the appropriate second-order conditions, this would generate the maximum net revenue, because the only flat spot on a hill is at the top!

Cournot's revenue function is perfect: price times quantity is indeed sales. The cost analysis, however, suffers from a critical error. His discussion of $\varnothing'(D)$ gives the reader the impression that Cournot is examining marginal cost in terms of the derivative of the cost function. Careful reading, however, shows that this is not the case. Cournot writes,

> [For manufactured articles] when D increases $\varnothing'(D)$ is a decreasing function. This comes from better organization of the work, from discounts on the price of raw materials for large purchases, and finally from the reduction of what is known to producers as 'general expense'. . . . It may happen, however, even in exploiting products of this nature [i.e., manufactured as opposed to agricultural], that when the exploitation is carried beyond certain limits, it *induces higher prices for raw materials and labour*, to the point where $\varnothing'(D)$ again begins to increase with D.[9]

Thus, Cournot's 'cost function' is simply the sum of each input's price (w_i) times the total amount of each input (x_i) used, $\Sigma w_i x_i$. Moreover, $\varnothing'(D)$ is the increase in $\Sigma w_i x_i$ when more output is produced. The reason $\varnothing'(D)$ falls is that quantity discounts and other measures lead to decreases in input prices. Cournot did not realize that the optimal rate of input usage (the cost minimizing input usage) is what x must be evaluated at. A true cost function plots the cheapest way to produce any given level of output. Marginal cost increases solely because marginal productivity falls; input price remains constant. Cournot believes, incorrectly, that the change in w_i will cause a movement along the cost function. In fact, a change in input price will shift the cost function. Cournot understood none of these subtleties, but given that he was decades ahead of his time, this is to be expected.

It was Alfred Marshall who, 40 years later, combined Cournot's novel view of the firm's product market (in terms of revenue and cost functions, and optimization theory) with the principle of substitution. Marshall realized that

> in calculating the expenses of production of a commodity we must take account of the fact that changes in the amounts

75

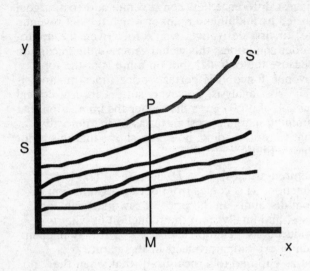

Figure 3.1 Marshall's rising supply curve

produced are likely, even when there is no new invention, to
be accompanied by changes in the relative quantities of its
several factors of production . . . As far as the knowledge and
business enterprise of the producers reach, they in each case
choose the factors of production which are best for their
purpose; the sum of the supply prices of those factors which
are used is, as a rule, less than the sum of the supply prices
of any other set of factors which could be substituted for
them.[10]

The wording is correct, but Marshall's graphical exposition, which
he relegated to a footnote, did not exactly present the entire
picture. In Figure 3.1, *SS'* is the average cost curve, and *MP* is
the average cost of producing *M* units. Marshall emphasizes that
the general upward slope is due to diminishing productivity, not
increasing input price. Even though input prices remain constant,
increasing output requires greater than proportional increases in
inputs, resulting in increasing per unit cost.[11]

Marshall understood that the cost function was more than $\Sigma w_i x_i$;
however, he did not utilize this knowledge to solve the firm's
output side maximization problem. Nor did he explicitly show the
difference and relationship between average and marginal costs.

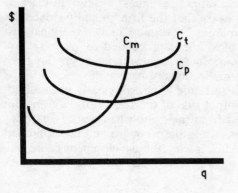

Figure 3.2   Harrod's short-run firm cost structure

This final step in the development of the output side, made possibly only after the cost function was correctly derived, is the presentation of the correctly solved revenue and cost functions in its modern graphical exposition. Credit here is given to Roy Harrod and Jacob Viner.

Harrod accurately portrays the short-run cost structure of a firm, distinguishing between fixed, marginal, and average costs.[12] In Figure 3.2, C_m is marginal cost, C_t is average total cost, and C_p is average variable cost.

Viner, in his now-famous 'draftsman's problem' article, also correctly analyzed the short-run cost structure of a firm (Figure 3.3).[13]

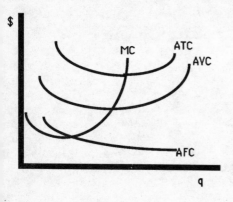

Figure 3.3   Viner's short-run firm cost structure

Both discussed the effect on net revenues of different market-given prices. They were aware that the firm should produce the level of output at which marginal revenue equalled marginal cost in order to maximize profits. Viner proceeded to graph several long-run situations (constant, increasing, and decreasing long-run costs) and to discuss the implications of each type.

Cournot, Marshall, Harrod, and Viner all clearly understood, to varying degrees, the output side of the theory of the firm. But it is just as clear – at least from their published work – that they had no idea of its relationship to the isoquant and factor market optimization problems. After tracing the development of the isoquant characterization, we will begin our analysis of the path toward synthesis.

The isoquant side – historical development

The historical development of the isoquant characterization (that is, the choice of the cost-minimizing input combination) is clear. All that was needed was for someone to realize that the consumer's problem (maximizing utility subject to a budget constraint) is identical, mathematically speaking, to the producer's isoquant side problem.

The earliest graphical exposition of indifference curve analysis is found in Irving Fisher's *Mathematical Investigations in the Theory of Value and Prices* (1892). Fisher defines indifference curves, discusses the budget constraint, and solves the optimization problem (Figure 3.4).[14]

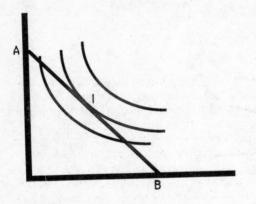

Figure 3.4 Fisher's indifference curve analysis

[The consumer] will select his combination in such a manner as to obtain the maximum total utility, which is evidently at the point I where *AB is tangent to an indifference curve.*[15]

It was not until 1913, however, that W. E. Johnson perfectly described – verbally, graphically, and mathematically – the neo-classical consumer utility theory. More importantly, for our purposes, he included a section on the producer's problem of maximizing output subject to a cost constraint. Let

$$p = f(a, b, c, \ldots) \qquad (n\text{-factors})$$

where

$$a\alpha + b\beta + c\gamma + \ldots = \mu, \quad [\mu = \text{given total cost}]$$

$Dp = 0$ gives

$$df/Da + df/Db + df/Dc + \ldots = 0,$$

$D\mu = 0$ gives

$$\alpha Da + \beta Db + \gamma Dc + \ldots = 0.$$

This gives

$$(\kappa.df/da - \alpha)Da + (\kappa.df/db - \beta)Db \ldots = 0,$$

for arbitrary increments $Da, Db, \ldots$.
Hence κ is determined by the *n*-equations,

$$\frac{\alpha}{df/da} = \frac{\beta}{df/db} = \ldots = \kappa \qquad [1]$$

These *n*-equations together with

$$a\alpha + b\beta + c\gamma + \ldots = \mu,$$

determine the $(n + 1)$ quantities $\kappa, a, b, c, \ldots$.[16]

Equation [1] is the familiar cost-minimizing first-order condition – the ratio of input price to marginal productivity must be equal across all factors. By changing the level of output, Johnson could find the cost-minimizing levels of input use for each output level, a creature better known as the 'least-cost expansion path'.

With the simple extension of indifference analysis to the production side, the isoquant characterization of the producer's optimization problem was complete. The next, and crucial, step, requiring a higher level of understanding, was the union of the three facets of the modern theory of the firm into the coherent whole it is today.

The entrepreneur in microeconomic theory

The entire system integrated – precursors

In this section, we review the first attempts at integrating the different facets of the theory of the firm. The failure to mix correctly the three optimization problems into a coherent whole marks the work of those labelled 'precursors'.

Amazingly, Leon Walras, as early as 1874, was the first to undertake this task. His grasp of the isoquant and factor market sides was adequate; however, a critical error in the output side showed he was just short of full understanding. Although Walras correctly derived the firm's cost structure, he incorrectly solved for the optimal rate of output. During the following years, the three facets of orthodox microeconomic production theory were refined and disseminated throughout the profession, but the pieces were kept apart.

It was not until 1924 that Arthur L. Bowley made the second attempt at integration. John R. Hicks, writing in 1932, also came close to synthesizing the different facets of the theory of the firm. Bowley and Hicks, however, closely followed Walras' path and unfortunately, made the same fundamental error.

The final precursor is Joan Robinson. By analyzing a single firm and thereby avoiding a general equilibrium framework, Robinson managed to sidestep the obstacle that plagued her predecessors. She failed, however, to analyze all three facets, focusing only on the output and factor market sides.

The analysis of the precursors to a full understanding of the theory of the firm proceeds in chronological order. We will review in turn, the production theories of Walras, Bowley, Hicks, and Robinson. However, before we begin, a brief aside on the distinction between general and partial equilibrium in the context of the theory of the firm will shed light on the error made by Walras and his followers.

A short essay on general and firm equilibrium

Equilibrium, in its broadest sense, means no tendency to change. It is described as a position of rest or lack of movement. Change can only occur through some exogenous shock which is then said to 'disturb the equilibrium'. A useful distinction, however, can be and has been drawn between general and partial equilibrium. General equilibrium is a Walrasian device; partial equilibrium has a long history, but its most influential user is Marshall. The distinction rests on the scope of the variables being considered. When all variables are at rest, there is said to be a general equilibrium; when only a particular subset exhibits no tendency to change, there is a partial equilibrium.

The general equilibrium analysis considers all variables and all interrelationships between markets. An exogenous change in one area will be felt eventually throughout the entire system because the system is joined through a complex series of feedback mechanisms and loops. The analysis of a given shock is not complete until all initial and subsequent effects have worked their way through the system and all endogenous variables are at rest.

On the other hand, partial equilibrium analysis, as Schumpeter explains, is based on the principle of the negligibility of indirect effects:

> When we are interested in those economic phenomena that can be observed in small sectors of the economy, for example in individual 'industries' of moderate size and, in the limiting case, in individual households or firms, we may assume that nothing that happens in these small sectors exerts any appreciable influence on the rest of the economy.[17]

Thus the feedback mechanisms (or indirect effects) are assumed away and the analysis is restricted to a much smaller subset of variables.

The particular subset of variables of concern in the theory of the firm include the quantity of output produced by each firm and the quantities of the inputs hired by each firm. When the optimal values of these endogenous variables are found and there is, therefore, no tendency to change, there is said to be a 'firm equilibrium'. General equilibrium, on the other hand, means that, in addition to equilibrium for output and input levels for the firm, all prices must be in a state of rest. Prices are no longer parameters or givens, but are endogenous variables.

For the theory of the firm, general equilibrium necessarily implies that all firms must be in equilibrium, but a particular firm and industry can be in equilibrium within a general *dis*equilibrium environment. Firm equilibrium simply means that the firm is at its maximum profit position; no available, internal adjustment can increase profits. Typically, this idea is posited in an environment of zero profit, where price equals minimum average cost, but this need not be so. And we shall see below that it was this misunderstanding which made it impossible for Walras and his followers to integrate the pieces of the theory into a unified, consistently related set of postulates and results.

In Figure 3.5 the i-th firm is in firm equilibrium, but not in

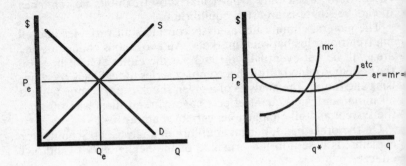

Figure 3.5 Firm equilibrium within a general disequilibrium
environment

general equilibrium. Clearly, there is nothing the firm can do to
improve its position; thus there is no tendency to change.

General equilibrium means that all parts of the system exhibit
no tendency for change, either through internal or external adjustment. Thus general equilibrium is often described as a long-run
equilibrium because all factors of production are variable and
have been allocated to their highest paid uses. In Figure 3.5, there
is no internal adjustment the firm can make that will improve its
position. Clearly, however, external adjustments are in order.
This firm is making a non-zero profit that will be competed away
by the entry of rivals. This tendency toward change (entry
increasing supply and falling price) is indicative of the present
general disequilibrium environment. Changing product prices will
cause other product prices to change (insofar as goods are substi
tutes or complements), which in turn will trigger changes in
demand curves and further price changes. The number and type
of feedback mechanisms are almost unimaginable, but we know
that a general equilibrium will be reached when all variables are
at rest.

The key point is that the distinction between general and firm
equilibrium is determined by the scope of the analysis. General
equilibrium analysis implies that all variables are endogenous
while firm equilibrium analysis assumes prices to be given. Gen
eral equilibrium is a much broader type of study, and one that
necessarily implies firm equilibrium. It must be emphasized, how
ever, that the reverse does not hold: a partial equilibrium says
nothing about the general equilibrium state of the system. It will

be clear below that it was this point that was missed by Walras and those who followed in his footsteps.

Leon Walras

Leon Walras presented what became neoclassical general equilibrium theory in his greatest work, *Elements d'économie pure*. (The first edition of the *Elements* appeared in 1874; the final, definitive edition was published in 1926, but all the changes had been made by 1902. William Jaffe's 1954 English translation of the definitive edition provides excellent translator's notes and cross-references to other editions.) Importantly, Walras' theory of the firm was tied inextricably to his general equilibrium theory. He analyzed the firm in a perfectly competitive, long-run, general equilibrium environment. Walras concluded that such an environment will generate three results: 'the demand and supply of each [1] service or [2] product are equal and [3] the *selling price* of each product is equal to the *cost of production*, i.e. the cost of the productive services employed.'[18]

But, and this is the key, at the optimal rate of output, price equals average cost only as a result of general equilibrium. The theory of the firm can be analyzed (as discussed in the previous section) in a much less restrictive theoretical environment – one in which a firm equilibrium can be established. In the firm equilibrium analysis, the relationship between output price and average cost is irrelevant to the determination of the profit-maximizing output level. Walras missed this crucial point and argued that

> if the selling price exceeds the cost of the productive services for certain firms and a *profit* results, entrepreneurs will flow toward this branch of production or expand their output, so that the quantity of the product [on the market] will increase, its price will fall, and the difference between price and cost will be reduced.[19]

Clearly, Walras believes that it is output price compared to average cost that determines the optimal rate of output. But just as clear is the error in this reasoning: it is the equality of marginal cost to the given price that determines the profit-maximizing rate of output. Walras' statement that producers will 'expand their output' in response to a price greater than average cost situation is simply incorrect.

A closer examination of Walras' work will show what he understood and where he went wrong. Walras begins by considering the isoquant side optimization problem (that is, to minimize the cost of producing a given level of output):

Let us insert a *predetermined quantity* to be manufactured Q of the product (B) into the cost of production equation . . .

$$Q_B = TP_t + PP_p + KP_k + \ldots \qquad (1)$$

Inserting Q now into the production equation, we have . . .

$$Q_B = \emptyset(T,P,K, \ldots) \qquad (2).^{20}$$

Walras then proceeds to derive correctly the conditions for the cost-minimizing input combination:

$$\frac{P_t}{\delta\emptyset/\delta T} = \frac{P_p}{\delta\emptyset/\delta P} = \frac{P_k}{\delta\emptyset/\delta K} = \ldots$$

Importantly, Walras believes these first-order conditions are a result of competitive, general equilibrium market forces. He concludes:

> Thus: 1. Free competition brings the cost of production down to a minimum.
> 2. In a state of equilibrium, when cost of production and selling price are equal, the prices of the services are proportional to their marginal productivities.[21]

The modern reader should see immediately the error in these propositions. The isoquant side has nothing whatsoever to do with the output market structure; it is purely a cost-minimization problem depending on the production technology, input prices, and a given level of output. Schumpeter notes that 'since firms will always try to minimize total cost, whatever their output, propositions (1) and (2) hold also for outputs other than the equilibrium output of pure competition'.[22]

In his translator's notes, Jaffe agrees with Schumpeter and argues that Walras' error stemmed from a mistaken view of the effects of competition:

> Its [$MP_i/w_i = MP_j/w_j$] validity does not depend – as Walras apparently imagined – on any assumptions regarding the competitiveness of the product market . . . [Walras' solution] was vitiated by his confusion of the problem of minimizing cost with that of equating minimum cost to selling price.[23]

What exactly was Walras', confusion? In a nutshell, his solution to the output side optimization problem was incorrect. Walras solved for the wrong 'predetermined quantity' that cost was to be minimized for. He chose, not that quantity where marginal cost (MC) equals price (P), but that quantity where average cost (AC) equals price.

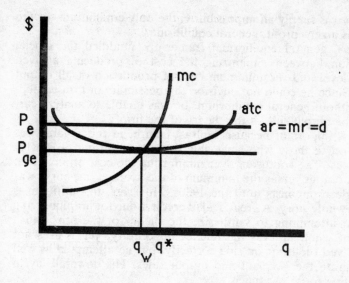

Figure 3.6 Walras' confusion on the output side

Under the special circumstances of a perfectly competitive, general equilibrium, Walras is correct, but for the wrong reason. The profit-maximizing firm never chooses the quantity at which average cost equals price; it always chooses the quantity where marginal cost equals price (MC = P, given that it can cover its variable costs). This is the firm equilibrium position. In general equilibrium, the firm does nothing differently; it chooses that level of output where marginal cost equals the given price. A further condition is imposed upon it by general equilibrium, that is, that average cost equals price (AC = P).

In Figure 3.6, we can compare the correct and Walrasian solutions to the output side maximization problem.

The equality of marginal cost and price determines the profit-maximizing level of output (q^*); average cost is clearly irrelevant. No other value of q can improve profits; thus q^* is the optimal and equilibrium value of output. Walras, however, simply could not see this solution as possible. He insisted, as we have noted above, that any situation where price was greater than average cost would lead firms to 'expand their output', which would cause 'prices to fall'. This would continue until profits were driven to zero. Therefore the equilibrium level of output for the firm (q_w) had to be where the long-run, general equilibrium price (p_{ge}) equalled average cost. Thus for Walras the firm equilibrium position was simply an impossibility; the only equilibrium for the firm was a zero profit, general equilibrium.

Walras' general equilibrium framework muddled the crucial distinction between minimizing the cost of producing a given output level and the minimum cost of production of all output levels. Since he could not envision the possibility of firm equilibrium without general equilibrium, he was unable to analyze correctly the output side of the theory of the firm.

This is important because Walras' failure, in this regard, was passed on to those who were able to understand him – Bowley and Hicks. The confusion over minimizing the cost of any given level of output versus the minimum of the average cost curve was to puzzle economists until the 1930s. However, this criticism is not the whole story. A great deal of credit is due for his pioneering work in attempting to synthesize the theory of the firm into a coherent whole. It was the nineteenth century, yet Walras not only solved the isoquant side correctly, but he attempted as well to integrate the isoquant and output sides. His downfall lay in attempting to do too much.

Arthur Bowley

Arthur Bowley's contribution to economic theory lies in the rewording and dissemination of the Walrasian mathematical, general equilibrium system to a wider English-speaking audience. By his own admission, *The Mathematical Groundwork of Economics* (1924) was not an original work.

> I have attempted to reduce to a uniform notation, and to present as a properly related whole, the main part of the mathematical methods used by Cornot, Jevons, Pareto, Edgeworth, Marshall, Pigou and Johnson. . . . I have not intended to advance any new theorems in economics, nor do I claim any originality in mathematical results.[24]

It is interesting that Walras was omitted from the list of mathematical economists of the period, especially since Bowley's book draws heavily on the *Elements*. In any case, Schumpeter credits Bowley with making 'Walras' equilibrium system internationally accessible'[25] and with introducing 'the Walras-Pareto system in textbook form'.[26]

Once again we will focus on the production and cost relationships that are the theory of the firm, highlighting especially the attempt at synthesis. Bowley, after analyzing the consumer's optimization problem (using indifference analysis), naturally turns to the isoquant side. Analyzing a given production function, $x =$

$F(y_1, \ldots, y_s, \ldots, y_w)$, given input prices, and given total cost, $p'x$ (where p' is average cost); Bowley has the producer choose the rate of input use that minimizes p'. This unfamiliar and somewhat tortured presentation is correct in this case (the isoquant side), but it later leads to confusion and error. Given his optimization problem, Bowley correctly derives the first-order conditions:

$$\frac{1}{w_1}F_{y1} = \ldots = \frac{1}{w_s}F_{ys} = \ldots = \frac{1}{w_v}F_{yv}$$

He then presents an example with a production function,

$$x = 2y_1^2 + 3y_1y_2$$

and input prices, $w_1 = \$2$ and $w_2 = \$1$. Given $x = 10$, he correctly solves for y_1^* and y_2^*; showing the solution to this isoquant side example graphically and mathematically.

By altering the given level of output, he correctly derives the total cost function (or what he mistakenly calls the 'supply curve' – which we discuss further below). He discusses increasing, constant, and diminishing returns on the cost side, showing the marginal cost's relationship to average cost in each case.

Bowley then turns to the factor market. At this point, his fatal weakness – the confusion between minimizing cost for any given output and the zero-profit (price equals minimum average cost) condition – becomes apparent. Bowley forces the firm to be in a zero-profit position because he believes, mistakenly, that the optimum output will be found at such a point. Bowley simply minimizes the cost of production of the output level at which total revenue equals total cost. Like Walras, he chose the wrong level of output, that is, an output level other than that which maximizes profits.

Evidence of Bowley's confusion can be seen by applying his solution to his previous example. The production function will obviously not satisfy second-order conditions for a maximum since it exhibits increasing returns to scale. In other words, as Bowley correctly showed, average and marginal costs will fall throughout. Hence, the profit maximizing rate of output is infinity. On the factor market side, this conclusion is also quickly reached since the marginal product of y_1 is an increasing function and the marginal product of y_2 is a constant.

Bowley reaches a determinate solution by forcing the firm to produce where profits are zero and adding the constraint that this rate of output be produced by the least-cost combination of inputs. On the factor market side, Bowley chooses y_i ($i = 1, 2$), where

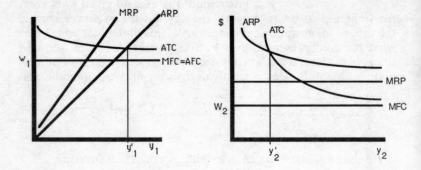

Figure 3.7 Bowley's factor market side solution

the average revenue product equals the average total cost (Figure 3.7). This zero-profit constraint also appears on the output side, where quantity is chosen so that average cost equals price (Figure 3.8).

Bowley's confusion is further illustrated by his terminology. For Bowley, the supply curve is the average cost curve because the firm determines its level of output by setting average cost equal to a given price. This, of course, is incorrect because the firm produces where marginal cost equals price and, therefore, the supply curve is the marginal cost curve. This error shows how strongly Bowley insisted on the zero-profit condition and how this stipulation on general equilibrium made it impossible for him to reach the correct solution.

We can see how closely Bowley followed Walras' footsteps; he made the exact same error. Instead of solving for the profit-maximizing level of output, Bowley's firm chose the zero-profit level of output. These two output solutions would coincide only if the firm were in a general equilibrium environment – a condition that need not hold for the theory of the firm to be applicable.

Bowley does get credit for trying to tie the various pieces together. His explicit derivation of the cost function is excellent work. But he did not understand how the optimal choices from the three optimization problems were consistently tied together. It would be another ten years before that task was accomplished.

John R. Hicks

J. R. Hicks has the unique distinction of writing two books, *The Theory of Wages* (1932) and *Value and Capital* (1939), during a

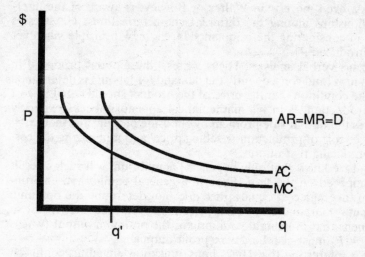

Figure 3.8 Bowley's output side solution

period in which work on the theory of the firm was at its peak. Consequently, a somewhat confusing situation arises: 'early' Hicks (whom we will examine here) followed the Walras-Bowley confusion, while 'late' Hicks (examined in the next section) was on the ground floor of the construction of the correct presentation.

The Theory of Wages opens with what Hicks calls a 'conventional proof' of the marginal productivity theorem:

> The number of labourers which an employer will prefer to take on is that number which makes his profit a maximum, and that number is given by the equality of wages to the marginal product of the labour employed.[27]

Hicks believes that the 'conventional method of proof' (that is, the factor market side) is useful in some situations, 'but other applications come out much more clearly if we adopt another way of looking at it (which is quite consistent with the first).'[28] This alternative method is the isoquant side. Hicks presents an excellent verbal exposition of the problem of minimizing cost given a level of output. In his mathematical appendix, he shows how 'we can construct a (very specialized) cost curve for the firm, giving the cost per unit of producing various outputs.'[29]

Once again we are at the brink of full-scale understanding, of total integration, of the theory of the firm still taught today. But just as before, the output side problem is solved incorrectly.

Hicks, even more than Walras or Bowley, is aware of the inter-relationships among the different characterizations. He stresses that in considering the isoquant side, 'no new principle whatever is introduced'.[30]

In his verbal analysis, Hicks writes, 'the amount produced in each firm (and consequently the demand for labour) is determined by the condition that the price of the product should equal its cost of production'.[31] In his mathematical appendix, Hicks explicitly solves the output side problem by choosing output such that '$\pi_x = p_x$, i.e. cost of production = selling price' and minimizing the cost of producing that output.[32]

But we know that only in general equilibrium will such a result be imposed on the firm. Even in a general equilibrium environment, average cost equals price does not determine the optimum output – marginal cost equals price is the relevant rule. It just so happens that in general equilibrium, the optimum output (where $MC = P$) must also be a zero-profit output.

It is interesting that Hicks himself acknowledged his confusion in a revised edition published 30 years later. Hicks understood that any given output must be produced at minimum cost. He also believed, mistakenly, that the minimum cost point of the average cost curve determined the optimum output: 'What I had not realized is that minimum cost, in this sense [min AC], is not a condition of maximizing profits.'[33]

Thus Hicks followed Walras and Bowley down the same wrong path. The pieces were all there, but it was almost as though they were trying to accomplish too much at one time. Instead of focusing on an individual firm's optimization problem, the Walrasian line of thought sought to find a firm and general equilibrium solution simultaneously. The resulting error, in choosing the optimal rate of output on the output side, prevented the correct exposition of the consistent, integrated theory of the firm.

Joan Robinson

Unhindered by the general equilibrium framework that led to the 'minimum cost' confusion, Joan Robinson clearly understood the role marginal relationships played in optimization. In *The Economics of Imperfect Competition* (1933), she presented the dual problems of maximizing profit from the output and factor market sides. Robinson, perhaps most renowned for the introduction of the marginal revenue curve, presented the perfect and imperfect (less than infinitely elastic demand or supply functions) output and factor market cases in excellent fashion.

Robinson explicitly ties the firm's profit position on the output

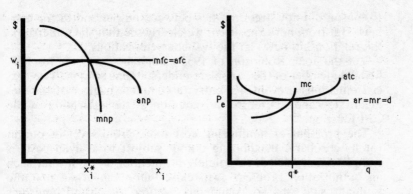

Figure 3.9 Robinson's factor market and output side solution

side with its counterpart on the factor market side. Though typically very clear, her use of a series of marginal and average productivity curves demands concentration (in particular, average net productivity is the value of the average product less the per unit factor cost of the other factors at their optimal rates of usage). Close attention, however, shows her analysis to be correct. Robinson's work clearly demonstrates that the firm's profit can be analyzed from either the output or factor market side, since the two must yield equivalent results. A true breakthrough, this shows the necessary relationship between these two optimization problems.

> [W]hen a perfectly competitive industry is in full equilibrium, each firm produces such an output that the average cost of production per unit of output is at a minimum, and we now see that the number of men employed by each firm is such that average net productivity per man is at a maximum.[34]

In graphical terms, Robinson is comparing the output market with the factor market in a long-run competitive equilibrium environment (Figure 3.9).

Robinson clearly understood the marginal relationships that determine the optimum position: marginal revenue and marginal cost for the optimum output; marginal revenue product and marginal factor cost for the optimum factor use. The average values determine the firm's profit position: average revenue and average cost for the output side; average net productivity and average factor cost for the factor market side.

Since she was focusing on the effects of market power (that is comparing perfect with monopoly or monopsony markets),

Robinson did not stress the ties between output and factor markets. But from her exposition, we clearly see that she understood the relationship between the two characterizations.

Yet the Joan Robinson of 1933 cannot be considered a fully fledged member of the 'complete understanding school'. Two crucial omissions prevent her entry: a complete neglect of the isoquant side and, therefore, no mention of the derivation of the cost function.

The problem of minimizing cost for a given level of output (or its corollary, maximizing output subject to a given cost) is completely neglected. Absolutely no mention is made that such an optimization problem even exists. One can argue that the isoquant side was so completely ignored because Robinson's emphasis was on comparing different market structures. Although it is true that the output market structure has no effect on the isoquant side, monopsony certainly plays a role (leading to a concave relative factor price constraint).

This neglect of the isoquant side made it impossible for Robinson to derive the cost function showing the cost-minimizing input combinations for different levels of output. She simply presents the marginal and average cost curves, making no mention of their derivation. Robinson does discuss shifts in the cost curves in passing, noting that a change in factor price will shift the entire curve. But although she may have realized the implications, the failure to examine closely the nature of the cost function prevents a true integration of three facets of the theory of the firm into a cohesive whole.

To summarize, Walras, Bowley, and Hicks analyzed the isoquant, output, and factor market optimization problems that together form the theory of the firm. Their attempts at synthesis would have succeeded but for the confusion over producing at 'minimum cost'. Robinson had no such misunderstanding of the determination of optimum output (or input) levels. However, she neglected completely the isoquant side, thus preventing a synthesis of the three facets into a consistent whole.

Nevertheless, the work of these precursors is not to be slighted. In the early 1930s, the theory of the firm was poised to make the final leap and assume the form it has today. To those who made that jump, we now turn.

The entire system integrated – full understanding

By the mid-1930s, before the focus shifted entirely to macroeconomics and the war, a tremendous amount of work was being done on the theory of the firm. All sides were being investigated: the debate continued on increasing returns, Chamberlin's *Monopolistic Competition* focused on individual market power, and a theory of wages, and distribution in general, was being discussed. The names of those participating in the debate are too varied to allow for a comprehensive review. A general survey of the journals reveals an array of famous economists working on the theory of the firm in the 1930s: Allen, Bowley, Coase, Frisch, Georgescu-Roegen, Harrod, Hicks, Hotelling, R. F. Kahn, Kaldor, Knight, Leontief, H. L. Moore, Robbins, Robinson, Schneider, H. Schultz, Schumpeter, Viner, and Zassenhaus.

Our task is to find those responsible for the full integration of the three facets of the theory of the firm into what we now call the modern theory of the firm. The assignment is not an easy one because work on the theory of the firm was about to reach its critical mass – finding an individual at a particular point in time responsible for understanding, unifying and explaining the entire system is impossible. Simultaneous discovery was almost a certainty under the existing environment.

Credit for full understanding and presentation of the modern theory of the firm is given, in no particular order, to Paul Samuelson, Sune Carlson, Ragnar Frisch, R. G. D. Allen, J. R. Hicks, and Erich Schneider. Vilfredo Pareto, who followed Walras at Lausanne, can claim priority in developing the modern theory of the firm. However, his work, for a variety of reasons, was neglected and it is Samuelson *et al.* who gained widespread acceptance and understanding for the integrated theory. All of these men presented a synthesized theory of the firm in the period from 1936–39.

Not surprisingly, the analyses and results were very similar. All showed the three sides of the optimization problem facing the firm. They correctly presented, through graphs and mathematics, the various terms that have become part of orthodox microtheory: the least-cost expansion path, cost-minimizing input demand functions, second-order conditions for an optimum, and the like. They even began extensions on the analysis: for example, Samuelson's comparative static exercises and Schneider's poly-periodic production interval.

The crucial point, however, for our purposes is not the history per se, but that the modern theory of the firm was installed as a fundamental part of microeconomics during the modern microeconomic era. Orthodox microeconomic theory had changed from a basic Marshallian analysis to the Hicks-Allen-Samuelson theory of the firm. Modern microeconomists, led by a new generation of theorists, had reworked the neoclassical vision of the market system to include the modern theory of the firm as the linchpin of the explanatory mechanism.

Work proceeded rapidly on the properties of production functions (homogeneity, homotheticity, CES, and trans-log were soon to be keywords), on various market structures (monopsony, price discrimination), and on duality theorems. The thrust of the analysis became an examination of the properties of the model under various extensions and constraints.

The rise of the modern theory of the firm signalled the beginning of the modern microeconomic era. Orthodox microeconomics had undergone a shift in emphasis – a shift which, we will soon see, had a profound effect on the entrepreneur as an explanatory element in standard economic theory.

To conclude, this section was designed to trace the general development of the modern theory of the firm. The history of the modern theory of the firm is best described as a movement toward the integration of the isoquant, output, and factor market sides into a cohesive whole.

The factor market side had the earliest roots; classical economists placed diminishing returns at the centre of their analysis. Johann von Thunen precisely formulated the maximization conditions in 1826. Wicksteed and Wicksell polished and presented the graphical and mathematical expositions at the turn of the twentieth century. The output side was marked by the neglected work of Augustin Cournot in 1838 and revived in the Marshallian analysis. The modern presentation of the cost curves was given by Harrod and Viner in the early 1930s. W. E. Johnson simply borrowed the indifference analysis from consumer theory (originally formulated by Edgeworth and Fisher) to solve the firm's isoquant side problem.

The pieces were all laid out, all that remained was for someone to tie them together. This process was hindered greatly in the case of Walras, Bowley, and Hicks because of a fundamental misunderstanding. The cost function defines the minimum cost of producing any given output. It is true that for a firm to maximize profit, it must produce its chosen rate of output in a least-cost manner. But this is very different from saying the optimal output is that which can be produced at the minimum point of the average cost curve. The modern reader has no trouble understanding this distinction, which seems so very basic and routine. But to those initially grappling with the various facets of the theory, it was an impassable obstacle. The work of Joan Robinson focused attention on the ties between the factor market and output sides. The introduction of the marginal revenue curve forced all to realize that marginal considerations determine optimal choices.

From there, any one of several economists can be considered as having synthesized the parts into their present logically coherent whole – the modern theory of the firm. This was achieved in the late 1930s. By the middle of the twentieth century, an understanding of the interrelationships between the three facets had spread throughout the discipline. With the exception of Ronald Shephard's research in duality theory[35] (basically a shortcut to the traditional results), nothing new has been added. Once synthesized, the theory of the firm has remained virtually unchanged as one of the pillars of the orthodox theory of value.

Most importantly, standard microeconomic theorists had adopted the modern theory of the firm as a fundamental element in their explanation of the market system. The modern theory of the firm became orthodox microeconomic theory. The effect on the entrepreneur was substantial and devastating.

The first level of explanation – historical evidence

Having traced two intellectual histories in economics, those of the entrepreneur and the theory of the firm, we can begin the first level of explanation – a description of the disappearance of the entrepreneur. The goal is not a causal or motivational analysis, but an attempt to establish empirically that the theory of the firm was somehow responsible for the disappearance of the entrepreneur as an explanatory agent in the orthodox economic paradigm. The 'somehow', of course, is an interesting, important, and difficult question, but one that must be postponed until this first level of explanation is completed.

Chapter 2 showed that the entrepreneur did in fact disappear from orthodox economics during the modern microeconomic era. The first section of this chapter outlined the development of the theory of the firm during the neoclassical era. Importantly, the third phase of neoclassical theory, the modern microeconomic period, was ushered in by the integration of three optimization problems into the consistent whole we call the modern theory of the firm.

It is this relationship – the disappearance of the entrepreneur during the same era as the rise of the modern theory of the firm - that focuses attention on the modern theory of the firm. It is important to note that the entrepreneur was not neglected throughout the microeconomic era, but only since the development of the modern theory of the firm.

The argument can perhaps best be made simply by placing the histories of the entrepreneur and the theory of the firm side by side. Table 3.1 splits economic theory since 1800 into three parts; pre-neoclassical, early and mature neoclassical, and modern microeconomic theory. The early and mature neoclassical theories were grouped together for convenience and because many of the works spanned both periods.

The pre-neoclassical era saw the research into entrepreneurship dominated by the French tradition (Cantillon in 1755, Say and Dupuit). The theory of the firm, of course, could hardly be recognized at this time, but we have seen how Thunen and Cournot provided some of the early building blocks.

The early and mature neoclassical eras saw research into both entrepreneurship and the theory of the firm flourish. It is during this time that Marshall, Schumpeter, and Knight placed entrepreneurship at the head of their differing explanations of the market system. Concurrently, a diverse group of economists were grappling with the isoquant, output, and factor market sides of the theory of the firm. Importantly, note that the early and mature neoclassical research program and studies of entrepreneurship are not mutually exclusive. Marshall, Edgeworth, and Schumpeter, to name only three of almost the entire group, considered themselves neoclassical theorists *and* proponents of entrepreneurship as a necessary explanatory factor. Even the father of general equilibrium theory, Leon Walras, cannot be said to have ignored completely the importance of the entrepreneur.

The modern microeconomic era, however, marks a sudden, significant change from the earlier stages of neoclassical theory. Research into entrepreneurship, within the orthodox paradigm, disappears and the modern theory of the firm reaches its full development. Neither Samuelson, Hicks, nor Allen makes any mention of entrepreneurship; the focus is on the theory of the firm as a set of interlocking, internally consistent pieces.

Table 3.1 clearly shows the point being made: the decline of the entrepreneur as an explanatory factor in orthodox economic theory coincides exactly with the rise of the modern theory of the firm. Or, even more simply put: the left-hand corner of Table 3.1 is blank.

Note, once again, that it is not neoclassical theory as a monolithic whole that neglects the entrepreneur. In general, early neoclassicals discussed entrepreneurship and worked on the individual pieces of the firm. Mature neoclassicals discussed entrepreneurship and, except for Bowley and 'early' Hicks, continued to view the theory of the firm in separate parts; modern microecon-

Research into Entrepreneurship (chapters 1 and 2)	Development of the Theory of the Firm (chapter 3)
	Pre-Neoclassical Theory
1800	
Say -- entrepreneur as coordinator	
	Thunen -- verbal exposition of the factor market side
1850 Dupuit -- entrepreneur as uncertainty bearer	Cournot -- first attempt at the output side
	Early and Mature Neoclassical Theory
1875	Walras -- the first "precursor"; failed to solve correctly the output side
1900 Edgeworth -- entrepreneur as coordinator	Edgeworth and Fisher -- graphical exposition of the consumer choice problem
Marshall -- the great eclectic; entrepreneur as coordinator, innovator, arbitrageur	Marshall -- understood production and cost relationships
	Wicksteed -- graphical and mathematical exposition of the factor market side, but no optimization framework
The American School (Fisher, JBClark, Hawley, Taussig, Davenport, Fetter) -- great debate on the entrepreneur's role in an uncertain environment	Wicksell -- numerical example of the factor market side
	Johnson -- correct exposition of the isoquant side
Schumpeter -- entrepreneur as innovator	
1920 Knight -- entrepreneur as responsible decision maker in an uncertain enviroment	
Dobb -- entrepreneur as innovator	Bowley -- the first follower of Walras; a failed attempt at integration
Tuttle -- entrepreneur as responsible owner in an uncertain environment	
1930	"Early" Hicks -- the second follower of Walras; another failed attempt at integration
	Modern Microeconomic Theory
1935	Frisch, Schneider, Allen, Carlson, "Late" Hicks, Samuelson -- the correct integration of the three facets into a consistent whole
	Stigler -- an early (1942) introductory level exposition of the modern theory of the firm
1950	Shephard -- the application of advanced mathematics generating a "short cut" to the traditional results

Table 3.1 The historical evidence for the disappearance of the entrepreneur from microeconomic theory

omists neglected the entrepreneur and synthesized the three facets of the firm into a consistent whole. As long as the pieces remained in their separate boxes, research into entrepreneurial issues flourished. In the 1930s, economics witnessed the combination of the various parts of the theory of the firm and the simultaneous decline of the entrepreneur.

Furthermore, note the perfect match in the speeds of the two developments. The entrepreneur did not gradually fade from the scene; the modern theory of the firm, in its late stages, was not slowly developed. In our review of the history of the entrepreneur in microeconomic thought, we emphasized the rapidity of the entrepreneur's disappearance. During the early and mature neo-classical eras, Marshall, Schumpeter, and Knight reigned supreme; every microeconomist had the entrepreneur, outside of general equilibrium, playing crucial roles in their explanations of the market system. In a very short period of time, however, the entrepreneur was removed from the orthodox microeconomic story. In the historical development of the theory of the firm, we spoke of the theory reaching a 'critical mass' before exploding on the scene in the 1930s. We were unable to disentangle the actual fathers of the integrated theory and were forced to name six original synthesizers.

Here, we note the correlation between these rapid changes in the discipline. Not only did the entrepreneur disappear as the theory of the firm was integrated into a consistent whole, but as fast as he departed, the modern theory of the firm entered. The theory of the firm came in a rush and the entrepreneur was rejected, simultaneously, just as quickly.

In this section, we simply placed two histories side by side and noted a rather striking correlation: the development of the modern theory of the firm during the 1930s was directly accompanied by the disappearance of the entrepreneur from microeconomic theory. Furthermore, we noted that the speeds of these two rapid changes were also perfectly matched.

Conclusion

This chapter presented the 'first level of explanation' for the disappearance of the entrepreneur from microeconomic theory. The goal was not to find a rationale or motivation for the sudden omission of the entrepreneur from the orthodox explanatory scheme; it was, instead, simply to present the empirical observation that the entrepreneur disappeared as the modern theory of the firm appeared.

Having already traced the decline of the entrepreneur from the microeconomic research program in the modern microeconomic era in the previous chapter, a brief history of the theory of the firm composed the first part of this chapter. These two histories were the 'empirical' evidence used to support our description of what actually happened to the entrepreneur.

The essential points are captured in Table 3.1: research into entrepreneurship disappeared as suddenly as the theory of the firm arose. The perfect match of both the change in the content of orthodox theory and the speed with which the change took place was noted. Finally, it was emphasized that it was only during the modern microeconomic era that the entrepreneur disappeared from orthodox economic theory.

In a certain sense we have 'explained' why the entrepreneur disappeared, just as the eyewitness 'explains' by a simple retelling of what he has seen. But the story cannot end here, for the response to the eyewitness account is usually, 'But why did it happen?' There are, obviously, deeper levels of explanation; to the second of these, we now turn.

Notes

1 A fairly standard reference is James M. Henderson and Richard E. Quandt, *Microeconomic Theory*, 3rd edn (New York: McGraw-Hill, 1980; originally published 1958).

2 Joseph A. Schumpeter, *History of Economic Analysis* New York: Oxford University Press, 1954, p. 1028.

3 John R. Hicks, *The Theory of Wages* (New York: St. Martin's Press, 1963; originally published 1932), p. 234.

4 Johann von Thunen, *The Isolated State*, trans. by Carla M. Wartenburg, Peter Hall (ed.) (Oxford: Pergamon Press, 1966; originally published 1826), p. 230–2.

5 Philip H. Wicksteed, *An Essay on the Co-ordination of the Laws of Distribution* (London: Macmillan & Co., 1894), pp. 8–9.

6 Knut Wicksell, *Lectures on Political Economy*, vol 1, trans. by E. Classen (New York: Macmillan, 1934; originally published 1901), p. 112.

7 The sufficient condition at L^*, $\dfrac{\delta^2\pi}{\delta L^2} < 0$, is fulfilled.

8 Augustin Cournot, *Researches into the Mathematical Principles of the Theory of Wealth* trans. by Nathaniel T. Bacon (New York: The Macmillan Co., 1929; originally published 1838), p. 57.

9 Cournot, *Researches*, pp. 59–60 (emphasis added).

10 Alfred Marshall, *Principles of Economics*, 9th edn (New York: The Macmillan Co., 1961), pp. 340–1.

11 Marshall, *Principles*, p. 344.

12 Roy Harrod, 'Notes on supply', *Economic Journal* 40 (June 1930): 234.
13 Jacob Viner, 'Cost curves and supply curves' (1931), in J. Viner (ed.) *The Long View and the Short* (Glencoe, Ill.: The Free Press, 1958), p. 54.
14 Irving Fisher, *Mathematical Investigations in the Theory of Value and Prices* (New Haven: Yale University Press, 1925; originally published 1892), p. 68.
15 Fisher, *Mathematical Investigations*, p. 72.
16 W. E. Johnson, 'Pure theory of utility curves', *Economic Journal* 23 (1913): 506–7.
17 Schumpeter, *History of Economic Analysis*, p. 990.
18 Leon Walras, *Elements of Pure Economics*, trans. by William Jaffe (Homewood, Ill.: Richard D. Irwin, 1954), p. 42.
19 Walras, *Elements*, p. 225.
20 Walras, *Elements*, p. 384 (emphasis added).
21 Walras, *Elements*, p. 385.
22 Schumpeter, *History of Economic Analysis*, p. 1035.
23 Walras, *Elements*, Translator's Notes, p. 552.
24 Arthur L. Bowley, *The Mathematical Groundwork of Economics* (Oxford: Clarendon Press, 1924) pp. v–vi.
25 Schumpeter, *History of Economic Analysis*, p. 1149.
26 Schumpeter, *History of Economic Analysis*, p. 829.
27 Hicks, *The Theory of Wages*, p. 9.
28 Hicks, *The Theory of Wages*, p. 10.
29 Hicks, *The Theory of Wages*, p. 238.
30 Hicks, *The Theory of Wages*, p. 15.
31 Hicks, *The Theory of Wages*, p. 11.
32 Hicks, *The Theory of Wages*, p. 237.
33 Hicks, *The Theory of Wages*, p. 322.
34 Joan Robinson, *The Economics of Imperfect Competition*, 2nd edn (London: Macmillan, 1969; originally published 1933), p. 251.
35 Ronald W. Shephard, *Cost and Production Functions* (Princeton: Princeton University Press, 1953).

Chapter four

An explanation for the disappearance of the entrepreneur – the rationale

Introduction

In this chapter, we continue our tripartite explanation of the disappearance of the entrepreneur from microeconomic theory. We have shown in the previous chapter that the entrepreneur's departure coincided exactly with the arrival of the modern theory of the firm. This observation constituted our first level of explanation – a simple description of what actually happened.

Digging deeper, the question naturally presents itself: Why did the modern theory of the firm lead to the neglect of the entrepreneur as an explanatory element in microeconomic theory? The answer to this question, the second level of explanation, focuses on the theoretical assumptions inherent in the modern theory of the firm. The demarcation line between the mature neoclassical and modern microeconomic eras is determined by the development and acceptance of the modern theory of the firm. In the modern era, microeconomic theory, previously found in Marshall's *Principles* or the Lausanne school's general equilibrium analysis, became exclusively tied to the Hicks-Allen-Samuelson *et al.* exposition of the theory of the firm.

Importantly, the integration of the isoquant, output, and factor market sides (that is the development of the modern theory of the firm) required a set of assumptions that effectively precluded the use of a functional entrepreneurial role. This is our second level of explanation: the entrepreneur disappeared from microeconomic theory because the modern theory of the firm carried with it assumptions that were incompatible with the exercise of entrepreneurship.

Thus this chapter investigates why the entrepreneur disappeared from the point of view of the actual cause of the disappearance. If in the previous chapter we heard what amounted to an eyewitness account, then this chapter provides the coroner's testimony. The goal is to determine how the modern theory of the firm caused the disappearance of the entrepreneur.

The presentation of the second level of explanation is essentially a two-step process. The first section reviews the assumptions inherent in the modern theory of the firm. We then use the discussion in this section to show the impossibilty of introducing the entrepreneur into the modern theory of the firm because of the very nature of its assumptions.

The theoretical core of the modern theory of the firm

As is the case with any theoretical structure, a set of axioms (in the mathematical sense) are needed to provide a basis and starting point for further theoretical work. This section examines the axioms upon which the modern theory of the firm rests. Importantly, these fundamental postulates cannot be compromised; any factor that yields the slightest disagreement necessitates the rejection of the postulates or the factor in question.

By axiom or postulate we do not mean simply any condition or restriction. Microeconomic theorists often discuss, for example, convexity conditions, market power, and the degree of factor mobility. These assumptions, although indispensable to the correct working of the model, are strictly secondary.

The foundation of the modern theory of the firm, its basic axioms, consists of the following three fundamental concepts: the production function, the logic of rational choice, and perfect information. These three postulates form the core of the model and, most importantly – as the next section will show – are responsible for the removal of the entrepreneur from modern microeconomics. The key lies in the unyielding nature of these axioms; they effectively prevent the entrepreneur from playing a role in orthodox microeconomics.

In this section, we examine the three fundamental assumptions in the modern theory of the firm. The next section reviews the production function, focusing particularly on the fact that it exactly describes a firm's input-output possibilities. We then turn to the logic of rational choice, examining closely the framework of optimization which forms a fundamental part of the theory. Finally, we discuss the assumption of perfect information and review its role in the modern theory of the firm.

The production function

The first fundamental building block or postulate in the modern theory of the firm is the production function. Typically, the production function, $q = f(\underline{x})$, is said to be 'well-behaved', that is, it is

> assumed to be a single-valued continuous function with continuous first- and second-order partial derivatives. . . . It is assumed to be a regular strictly quasi-concave function when output is maximized or cost minimized, and a strictly concave function when profit is maximized.[1]

Much analysis and debate centers on the properties of the production function. The goal is to minimize the necessary assumptions of the production function in order to achieve greater generality. Our interest lies, however, not with the properties of the production function, but with the production function itself. The 'well-behaved' nature of the function is irrelevant – it is the use of a production relationship per se that is our main concern.

A production function describes the maximum output that can be generated from any given combination of inputs. Thus the production function presents the set of all technologically efficient production possibilities. Three important results flow from the use of the production function in the modern theory of the firm.

First, the production technology explicitly states not only the quantities of each factor necessary to make a given level of output, but also the type and function of each factor necessary to produce a given product. The production function gives the firm a complete and exact understanding of its input-output possibilities. Not only raw materials and manual labor are included, but also managers, supervisors, and decision-makers – every single factor necessary for production is explicitly designated. Each of these factors is involved in the production process in a particular, given way; that is, the function of each factor is tightly and precisely defined.

Second, use of the production function in the modern theory of the firm implies that every product has a given production relationship. All products are made by an explicitly given technological input-output relationship. At any point in time, the existing possibilities for output are known and given by a production function that corresponds to each product.

Finally, the use of the production function presents the firm, on the output and factor market sides, with an objective function to maximize. Profits are defined as revenues minus costs and revenues are, of course, product price times output. The production function tells the firm the output it can expect from any given combination of inputs. On the isoquant side, the production function provides a needed constraint in the optimization problem: minimize the cost of producing a given (by the production function) level of output. The elements in the production function, the output and factor levels, are the endogenous variables in each of the three optimization problems that comprise the modern theory of the firm.

Thus the production function is a crucial part of the modern theory of the firm. By exactly describing the firm's input-output possibilities, production function states the quantities and types of each factor necessary for production and the range of products available to the economy. In addition, the production relationship forms a key part of the firm's three optimization problems.

The logic of rational choice

The second fundamental postulate inherent in the modern theory of the firm involves rational choice. Specifically, the theory assumes that the firm rationally pursues its objectives – cost minimization and profit maximization. This axiom drives the model; the firm is exclusively engaged in solving the problem of how much output to produce and what types and quantities of factors to hire.

During the 1930s, orthodox microeconomic theory adopted Robbins' definition of economics: 'Economics is the science which studies human behavior as a relationship between ends and scarce means which have alternative uses.' [2] The modern theory of the firm, itself the foundation of modern microeconomics, naturally incorporates optimization into its framework. The firm, given its ends (the twin behavioral assumptions of cost minimization and profit maximization), applies the logic of rational choice: it chooses the optimal levels of the endogenous variables given its exogenous variables and constraints.

Let us assume a firm is an output and input price taker. Given its production function, it now must determine what level of output to produce and what quantities of inputs to hire. It is here that the logic of rational choice comes into play. The cost-minimization and profit-maximization assumptions give the firm the ends which it strives to reach.

The firm faces, as we have seen, three interrelated optimization problems. On the isoquant side, it chooses input levels ($\underline{x}$) such that cost ($\underline{w}'\underline{x}$) is minimized for a given level of output ($\bar{q}$):

$$\min C(\underline{x}) = \underline{w}'\underline{x} \tag{1}$$
$$\text{s.t. } \bar{q} = f(\underline{x})$$

On the output side, the firm chooses the level of output (q) that maximizes profit (total revenue minus total cost):

$$\max \pi(q) = Pq - C(q) \tag{2}$$

where, of course, the cost function, $C(q)$, indicates the least-cost combination of inputs for producing any given level of output.

Finally, on the factor market side, the firm chooses the level of inputs ($\underline{x}$) that maximize profit:

$$\max \pi(\underline{x}) = Pf(\underline{x}) - \underline{w}'\underline{x} \tag{3}$$

In each case, the firm's goal is presented as an optimization problem, either to minimize or maximize a given objective function. The relevant pieces (the production function and input and output prices) are assembled and ready to be used. It is casting the problem in an optimization framework, endowing the firm with the desire to reach a given goal and providing it with givens and choice variables, that determines the final equilibrium choices that will be made.

Applying the logic of rational choice has two crucial implications. First, it completely focuses the analysis on the endogenous variables. Once a problem is set up, the key is to find optimum levels of the choice variables, other considerations are irrelevant. Second, an optimization problem, in order to have a solution, must be close-ended, that is, it must contain all relevant information. For the modern theory of the firm, this means that the firm's production, output demand, and input supply functions must be known and given.

In this section, we have reviewed the second fundamental assumption of the modern theory of the firm – the logic of rational choice. By viewing the firm in an ends-means framework, the modern theory of the firm focuses exclusively on solving the firm's optimization problems. The firm is best characterized as a 'black box', or given production function, and the focus of attention is centered on the endogenous variables.

Perfect information

The final fundamental postulate in the modern theory of the firm is the assumption of perfect information or perfect knowledge. It is often criticized as the most unrealistic and restrictive theoretical assumption in the model, yet it cannot be relaxed.

For the modern theory of the firm, the perfect information assumption implies that each firm is completely aware of all considerations affecting its decisions. The firm is aware of its own product's production function, and that of every other commodity. It knows the quality and price of every product and factor of production. Furthermore, it knows these things, not only in the present, but also in the future.

Assuming perfect knowledge enables the firm to solve its optimization problem. It must have complete information about the production function, relevant prices, and any constraints. The perfect knowledge assumption guarantees these conditions are met. Without perfect information, the logic of rational choice, the application of the equimarginal principle, would be empty and useless.

Special mention should be made that the choice variables need not be deterministic; stochastic endogenous variables are permitted as long as their probability distributions are known. Thus Knight's distinction between risk and uncertainty is relevant here. The modern theory of the firm encounters no problems with risk, but it cannot operate in an environment characterized by true (or Knightian) uncertainty. The knowns must be known, either deterministically or probabilistically, for the logic of rational choice to function.

Therefore perfect knowledge is the third fundamental assumption of the modern theory of the firm. It guarantees that all information necessary for the solution of the firm's optimization problem is available. Without it, the theory would collapse.

To summarize in this section, we have presented three fundamental postulates of the modern theory of the firm: the production function, the logic of rational choice, and perfect information. Although further refinements and restrictions are needed to round out the model, these three assumptions form the core of the theory.

The production function is the backbone of the modern theory of the firm. It allows the firm to be viewed as an array of input-output possibilities. The logic of rational choice is the driving force in the theory. It provides the firm with objectives (typically, cost minimization and profit maximization) and endows the firm with the ability to strive rationally for its given goals. The final assumption, perfect information, ensures that all necessary data for the application of the ends-means framework are available.

These three assumptions form the foundation of the modern theory of the firm. Additional assumptions (market structure, production function restrictions, and the like) are added to generate 'testable predictions' through comparative static exercises. However, the broad outline of the theoretical structure is entirely captured within the three fundamental axioms discussed in this section.

The second level of explanation – the effects of the theoretical core

We are now prepared with an understanding of the postulates that form the foundation of the modern theory of the firm and ready to present our second level of explanation for the disappearance of the entrepreneur. Our goal is to provide a rationale for this disappearance; we want to go beyond mere description to analyze, in greater depth, the cause of neglect. The relevant question is: Why did the modern theory of the firm lead to the neglect of the entrepreneur as an explanatory element in microeconomic theory?

The answer is found by examining the theoretical core of the modern theory of the firm. It is the three postulates of this core that block the introduction of entrepreneurial considerations. The entrepreneur as innovator, uncertainty-bearer, coordinator, and arbitrageur is effectively removed from the modern theory of the firm, which is orthodox microeconomic theory, by the production function, the logic of rational choice, and the environment of perfect information.

It is important to emphasize the inability of the theory to compromise with any factor that disturbs the elements in the theoretical core. The entrepreneur, of course, is precisely such a factor and for this reason entrepreneurship could not co-exist with the modern theory of the firm. In this section, we will present this second level of explanation. Once again, our objective in this chapter is a rationale for and an in-depth account of the disappearance of the entrepreneur from microeconomic theory. The question of why the assumptions are the way they are is the subject of the next chapter – the motivation for the disappearance.

We present this second level of explanation simply by showing how the assumptions discussed in the previous section prevent the introduction of the entrepreneur in any of the four functional roles described in Chapter 1. To the first of these, innovation, we now turn.

The exclusion of the entrepreneur as innovator

Innovation is one of the more commonly accepted roles the entrepreneur has played in the history of economic thought. Schumpeter, of course, had one of the most appealing theories of the entrepreneur as innovator or creator of new combinations. In this role, the entrepreneur became the engine of the capitalist process.

For the modern theory of the firm, however, the entrepreneur as innovator is ruled out by the production function and the logic of rational choice. The production function presents the firm with an array of input-output possibilities. All possible outputs and their technologically efficient means of production are given by the production function. The logic of rational choice transforms the firm into an entity where choices are made in an environment of known parameters and objectives.

In the modern theory of the firm, the production relationship contains all of the endogenous variables. The production function manifests itself in the theory of the firm through the isoquant, the cost function, and the marginal (and average) factor productivity schedules. The logic of rational choice has the optimizing agent choose the factor uses that minimize cost, the output that maximizes profit, and the factor uses that maximize profit.

There is no orthodox theory of innovation within modern microeconomic theory because any such theory would clash with the modern theory of the firm's theoretical core. Of course, there can be innovation in terms of an exogenous shift in the production function, but a genuine theory of innovation focusing on the entrepreneur as creating internal change (*à la* Schumpeter) is incompatible with the modern theory of the firm.

New products are ruled out because the list of production functions and their corresponding products must be given and known in order for the logic of rational choice to allow the optimal values of the endogenous variables to be determined. Similarly, new production techniques involving cheaper or better methods of production are impossible given the fact that the production function establishes technologically efficient means of production. It is defined as the maximum output that can be obtained from any given combination of inputs.

Opening new markets, finding new sources of supply, or presenting new organizational forms are means of innovation that conflict with the logic of rational choice. All of the options have to be available to the decision-makers and their consequences must be known. The word 'new' is simply not allowed and, for this reason, innovation is simply beyond the scope of the analysis.

Any attempt to introduce innovation will cause the theory to collapse. Schumpeter noted that entrepreneurship, the generation of new combinations, could not exist within calculating personalities. There had to be an element of non-rational, instinctive decision-making. But it is precisely this element which crashes headfirst against the postulate of the ends-means framework. Innovation essentially implies that an agent has rejected the known means and is searching for something new, but this activity cannot be explained by the modern theory of the firm. Furthermore, it cannot be allowed to co-exist for it directly contradicts the logic of rational choice. Thus the entrepreneur as innovator cannot be an explanatory element within an orthodox microeconomics that accepts the modern theory of the firm.

The exclusion of the entrepreneur as uncertainty-bearer

In Chapter 1, we saw how a great deal of research into entrepreneurship had been done under the banner of uncertainty. Cantillon's speculator, Hawley's responsible owner, and Knight's responsible decision-maker were examples of theories placing emphasis on the entrepreneur's role in an uncertain environment. In each case, the entrepreneur acted as a buffer against the debilitating effects of an uncertain environment.

It is easy to see, however, that no such role need be played in the modern theory of the firm. The entrepreneur as uncertainty-bearer is removed by the assumption of perfect information. The firm exists in a world in which it has all necessary information, in which its expectations are exactly fulfilled. In such an environment, the optimizing agent can choose the optimum values of the endogenous variables.

The postulates of the logic of rational choice and perfect information straightforwardly remove any need for an entrepreneur as uncertainty-bearer. Since there is no uncertainty, such a function is superfluous.

Sometimes, attempts to incorporate uncertainty are characterized by the introduction of a random variable (for example, a random output demand function). As noted in the previous section, however, the randomness is limited to the case of risk, in which the probability distributions of all random variables are known. By optimizing expected values, the problem is essentially the same as in a world characterized by perfect knowledge. Davidson sees this point clearly.

> Replacing the concept of certainty by the concept of a known
> probability distribution merely replaces the assumption of
> perfect foreknowledge by the assumption that economic agents
> possess actuarial knowledge. In such a situation actuarial
> costs and benefits can be calculated, and the economic agent
> can act as if he possessed absolute foreknowledge.[3]

Not only is the entrepreneur as uncertainty-bearer superfluous,
but the attempt to introduce such an agent would sound the death
knell for the modern theory of the firm. Clearly, a truly uncertain
environment (in the Knightian sense) would spell the end of the
logic of rational choice. Radical uncertainty prevents the application of any optimization technique or rational, calculating solution algorithm; subjective opinion and intuition are the only
decision-making rules. Perfect information is a necessary part of
the modern theory of the firm. Without it, problems facing the
firm could not be cast and solved in an optimization framework.
With it, however, the entrepreneur as uncertainty-bearer is
needless.

The exclusion of the entrepreneur as coordinator

That the introduction of the entrepreneur as innovator or
uncertainty-bearer is incompatible with the assumptions inherent
in the modern theory of the firm does not seem controversial.
Neoclassical economists rarely, if ever, claim to include these
entrepreneurial roles in the theory of the firm.

The entrepreneur as coordinator and arbitrageur, however, is
another matter. Neoclassicals often describe the theory of the firm
headed by an entrepreneur as decision-maker, coordinating or
arbitraging. We will show that, like innovation and uncertainty-
bearing, these functions are unnecessary, given the postulates that
form the theoretical core of the modern theory of the firm.

'Coordination' is used in microeconomic theory in two senses:
as a necessary function in production and as a decision-making
activity. The first definition is simply another factor of production.
Managers and supervisors, just as other types of labor and raw
materials, are needed in production; they are factors x_i and x_j in
the input vector. There is no entrepreneurial activity involved in
such a task.

The latter definition is more widely used. In this sense, the
entrepreneur as coordinator is defined as the agent who chooses
and arranges the quantities of inputs hired:

> A firm is a technical unit in which commodities are produced.

Its entrepreneur (owner and manager) decides how much of and how one or more commodities will be produced, and gains the profit or bears the loss which results from his decision.[4]

But both tasks, arranging and choosing, are completely determined by the givens and objectives facing the optimizing agent. By giving the optimizer a production function, applying the logic of rational choice (including providing relevant givens and the two behavioral objectives of cost minimization and profit maximization), and perfect information, the problem is solved. In no real sense has any decision-making been exercised.

For example, on the isoquant side, the optimizing agent is said to determine 'how one or more commodities will be produced', but cost minimization immediately makes clear his only possible arrangement. In Figure 4.1 there is no 'choice' between input combinations A, B and C, given that the objective is to minimize cost. The optimizing agent must choose point B; there is no 'arranging' to be done.

For the same reason, 'deciding how much . . . will be produced' involves no real decision-making. The optimizing agent must

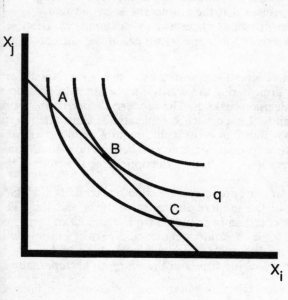

Figure 4.1 'Choosing' on the isoquant side

choose that quantity which maximizes profit; any other rate of output must be rejected.

It is a misuse of the word to argue the optimizing agent 'chooses' the levels and arrangement of the factors of production and output. The constraints so circumscribe the optimizer that only one true option is possible. Clearly, the lack of a viable alternative removes any notion of entrepreneurship as coordination, in the decision-making sense of the term, from the theory of the firm. True coordination, choosing and arranging the factors of production, requires the possibility of real error.

Thus, for example, Say's entrepreneur as coordinator was a special factor due to the presence of imperfect knowledge and an uncertain environment. Decision-making, combining, and supervising factors, involved choice among viable alternatives. The modern theory of the firm reduces coordination to, in Knight's terms, 'routine management' or, as Schumpeter said, 'mere management'. No real choice and therefore no real entrepreneurial activity is needed. Kay argues that the entrepreneur, in orthodox theory, is reduced to a mere computer:

> The assumption of rationality and the existence of marginalist
> profit-maximising rules couched in the perfect knowledge
> assumption, ensures that the entrepreneur has no real
> discretion over questions of resource allocation. . . . These
> same assumptions result in the treatment of the entrepreneur
> as an automaton. [5]

To allow the entrepreneur as coordinator to play a role, the theory must loosen its grip, easing the constraints in order to provide a true choice in decision-making. The modern theory of the firm however, can allow for no such complications. Any attempt to introduce the possibility of error would require ambiguity in one of the initial givens (production function, behavioral assumptions or perfect information), destroying the optimizing structure of the model.

Once again, an entrepreneurial function has come face to face with an axiom in the modern theory of the firm and lost. The entrepreneur as coordinator is barred from the modern theory of the firm by the logic of rational choice and perfect information. There can be neither real choice nor real decision-making in the modern theory of the firm and therefore no entrepreneur as coordinator.

The exclusion of the entrepreneur as arbitrageur

The second entrepreneurial role often cited in the modern theory of the firm is that of arbitrageur. Once again, we will argue that, in fact, there are no real arbitrage opportunities in the theory and thus no need for the entrepreneur as arbitrageur. Furthermore, the introduction of such an element is blocked by the postulates in the theoretical core.

In orthodox microeconomic theory, the entrepreneur, as the head of the firm, is supposedly an arbitrageur by virtue of his responsiveness to profit opportunities. In any industry where excess profits (defined as price greater than average cost) exist, firms enter, setting off a chain of events that eliminates the surplus. The reverse, exit in the face of loss, works much the same way. The entrepreneur is therefore the equilibrating agent, the means by which the economy reaches a long-run, general equilibrium.

This story is intuitively appealing, but false; seemingly consistent, but not. The only reason that a non-zero profit situation can ever arise in modern microeconomic theory (given free entry and exit) is due to factor immobility. Fixed factors of production prevent a firm from exiting when price falls below average cost and prevents existing firms from moving into excess profit markets. In time, as firms face long-run planning horizons (where all factors are variable), they move out of loss situations into excess profit industries. These adjustments continue until there are no excess profit markets – a long-run general equilibrium.

There is no need for any notions of arbitrage in this process. Time (removing the fixed factor constraint), free movement, and the profit-maximization objective will guarantee a long-run general equilibrium. No special entrepreneurial role need be played for the system to reach a position of rest.

The essence of arbitrage is reaction to ignorance. For some reason, a profitable situation is not being acted upon, resulting in an arbitrage opportunity. It is very much a disequilibrium phenomenon, for example, price such that quantity demanded is greater than quantity supplied, leaving a profit opportunity.

The firm in modern microeconomic theory is constantly in some sort of equilibrium. When in equilibrium, it maximizes profit, leaving no tendency for change. If excess profits exist at this point, it is not by virtue of a missed opportunity or a disequilibrium situation. Non-zero profit may exist, but only because of a binding constraint (for example, factor fixity), not because a Kirznerian entrepreneur failed to be alert to a profit opportunity. In fact, every agent in the modern theory of the firm knows where excess profits exist and is prevented from moving there only because of some constraint. Once all constraints are removed, profit will automatically disappear. No arbitrageur is eeded.

Once again, the introduction of an entrepreneur as arbitrageur is not only unnecessary, but would require changing axioms in the theoretical core. Thus, for example, Kirzner's entrepreneur as arbitrageur was alert to profit opportunities in the Austrian disequilibrium environment. He had the capacity to learn, to adjust in the face of new information, to realize errors are being made that will, when corrected, yield profit.

The modern theory of the firm has no room for such ideas. Even in firm equilibrium, if non-zero profits exist, it is certainly not due to inequality between quantities demanded and supplied. Neither are profits due to firms operating at non-profit maximizing levels of output because of some 'error' in choosing the level of output. Non-zero profit is only due to some kind of constraint, which will in time automatically correct itself.

The modern theory of the firm is a system guided by the logic of rational choice and aided by the assumption of perfect information. The modern orthodox explanation of market equilibrium is self-contained. Within this environment, entrepreneurs as arbitrageurs are simply redundant because some sort of equilibrium is always automatically reached. General equilibrium mechanically follows firm equilibrium as soon as the factor fixity constraint is removed. Furthermore, any attempt to include an entrepreneur as arbitrageur threatens the theoretical core that forms the heart of the modern theory of the firm.

To summarize, this section has shown that the entrepreneur, in any of his four fundamental roles, is not and cannot be a part of the modern theory of the firm. There is no innovation; the production function is given and the logic of rational choice demands that choices be made in an ends-means framework. There is no uncertainty-bearing; the present and future is known with absolute precision (or, what amounts to the same thing, all probability distributions are known) because there is perfect information. There is no coordination; 'choice' is exactly determined by the constraints and objectives. And, finally, there is no arbitrage; perfect information and the logic of rational choice ensure that all profit opportunities will be seized as soon as possible. Excess profits exist only because the factor fixity constraint makes adjustments impossible.

Furthermore, we have shown that any attempts to introduce

entrepreneurial considerations directly collide with one or more of the three postulates found in the theoretical core of the modern theory of the firm. The confrontation between the basic axioms and the entrepreneur leaves two possibilities: to accept the entrepreneur and reject the modern theory of the firm, or to reject the entrepreneur and maintain allegiance to the modern theory of the firm. The history of economic thought clearly shows the choice that was made.

It is important to note that the word 'entrepreneur' may be used by a modern microeconomic theorist, but only as one of many, equally important, factors of production. For the modern theory of the firm, entrepreneurship as innovation, true uncertainty-bearing, coordination, or arbitrage is absolutely superfluous – and to force the entrepreneur into the theory is absolutely devastating.

Conclusion

In this chapter, we presented our second level of explanation for the disappearance of the entrepreneur from microeconomic theory. In the first section, we reviewed three fundamental postulates in the modern theory of the firm: the production function, the logic of rational choice, and perfect information. These axioms form the backbone of the theory and, as shown in the second section, they leave neither room, nor allow for the possibility of including entrepreneurial considerations.

We have been discussing throughout this work the disappearance of the entrepreneur; perhaps, however, it would be more accurate to say that the entrepreneur became a powerless figurehead, overlooking a determinate model in which he played no part. Simply put, the firm runs itself. The modern orthodox description of a firm is that of a 'black box'. Inputs enter and, through the production function, are transformed into output. There is no place for any kind of entrepreneurial activity, defined as coordination, arbitrage, innovation, or uncertainty-bearing.

Modern microeconomic theory, at its most basic and powerful level of analysis, is the repeated application of optimization techniques (marginalism) to a wide variety of problems. The optimizing agent is in charge of choosing the optimum value of the variables under his control. Given an objective, the choice is instantly determined. The agent is not involved in the actual problem; he is somehow above the fray, looking down and picking the best configuration of choice variables.

Thus the consumer, given his tastes and preferences (by a utility function), prices and income, chooses the bundle of goods that maximizes his utility. The consumer per se is unimportant; the focus is on the chosen bundle of goods. In the modern theory of the firm, the entrepreneur is the optimizing agent, completely analogous to the consumer. Given a production function, input prices and output price, he chooses the cost-minimizing input vector, the profit-maximizing rate of output and the profit-maximizing input vector. The entrepreneur per se is unimportant; the focus is on the chosen combination of endogenous variables.

In fact, the role of the entrepreneur is even less important than that of the consumer. For the consumer, at least his preferences have some effect. Through their individual utility functions, consumers can (in the aggregate) exercise some measure of consumer sovereignty. The sum of their individual demand curves sends signals affecting production decisions. The entrepreneur in the modern theory of the firm has no such function. The production function is given to the entrepreneur; determined by exogenous forces.

In the 1930s, the entrepreneur received active consideration in the orthodox explanatory scheme. He then disappeared because the modern theory of the firm brought with it a set of postulates incompatible with the exercise of entrepreneurship. We have now completed our second level of explanation – an examination of the exact cause of the entrepreneur's disappearance. More than a description, we now know how the modern theory of the firm forced the removal of the entrepreneur; how the theory's core axioms prevent the introduction of the entrepreneur.

We still do not have, however, a motivating force behind the use of this particular set of basic postulates. In other words, we must answer the question; Why are the theoretical core axioms – the ones that prevent the entrepreneur from playing a role – the way they are? This is the subject of the next chapter, the third and final level of explanation.

Notes

1 James M. Henderson and Richard E. Quandt, *Microeconomic Theory: A Mathematical Approach* 3rd edn New York: McGraw Hill, 1980. p. 66.

2 Lionel Robbins, *Essays on the Nature and Significance of Economic Science* London: Macmillan, 1962, p. 16.

3 Paul Davidson, 'Post Keynesian economics', in Daniel Bell and Irving Kristol (eds) *The Crisis in Economic Theory* (New York: Basic Books, 1981), p. 160.

4 Henderson and Quandt, *Microeconomic Theory*, p. 64.

5 Neil M. Kay, *The Emergent Firm* (New York: St. Martin's Press, 1984), p. 57.

Chapter five

An explanation of the disappearance of the entrepreneur – the motivation

Introduction

We have shown, as a first level of explanation, that the rise of the modern theory of the firm exactly coincided with the disappearance of the entrepreneur from microeconomic theory. We then offered a deeper explanation, a detailed examination of the disappearance, arguing that the fundamental postulates of the modern theory of the firm prevent the introduction of entrepreneurial considerations. But we must go even deeper; once again we must ask 'Why?' The question before us is: Why are the axioms in the modern theory of the firm arranged in their present form?

The answer to this question is our third level of explanation – the motivation – for the disappearance of the entrepreneur. We know the entrepreneur was unable to maintain a place of importance in modern microeconomic theory because of its theoretical core. In this chapter, it is argued that the axioms in this core, in turn, are arranged in their present form because of internal consistency requirements. Thus the motivation behind the neglect of the entrepreneur lies in a need to maintain internal consistency within modern microeconomic theory.

In the battle between entrepreneurship and consistency, the latter emerged victorious. For microeconomic theory, any cost due to the neglect of entrepreneurship is effectively compensated by the gains from maintaining the complex, yet mutually reinforcing, set of interrelationships that comprise modern orthodox microeconomic theory. Consistency is a requirement; failure to meet it would destroy the theory. Thus the entrepreneur was removed as an explanatory element during the modern microeconomic era.

This chapter presents our third and final level of explanation. We have presented an 'eyewitness account' and a detailed rationale as the first two levels of explanation. Our goal now is to present

118

the detective's version of the disappearance. For this, we must provide a motive for the neglect of the entrepreneur. A theory's overriding need for internal consistency is the element that is proposed as the motivating force behind the disappearance of the entrepreneur from modern microeconomic theory.

The next section discusses the indispensable attribute of consistency in theoretical models. We then turn to the consistency properties of the modern theory of the firm, showing how the various pieces of the model fit together. Finally, we present our third level of explanation for the disappearance of the entrepreneur, arguing that consistency requirements won out over entrepreneurial considerations.

The importance of consistency

Although a review of the importance of consistency in a theoretical structure could easily lead to a full-scale methodological discussion, this is not our goal. Our objective is much more modest: simply put, it is argued that consistent or mutually compatible interrelationships within a theoretical structure are a prerequisite for a theory to be accorded serious consideration.

Formally, consistency

> requires that no axioms or relationships postulated within a theoretical structure may contradict other relations or axioms in the structure, and that no mutually incompatible theorems may be deducible from the postulated axioms and relations.[1]

Intuitively, logical consistency is the fitting of different pieces into a coherent whole. It is common-sense reasoning that a theoretical structure purporting to convey truth should not contradict itself. For this reason, Georgescu-Roegen argues that

> there can be no logical contradiction between any two factual propositions; in particular, the logical foundation of a science must be not only nonredundant – as warranted by the algorithm by which it is constructed – but also noncontradictory.[2]

The theorist, as a first step, checks that no contradictions can be found in his theoretical system. Karl Popper, discussing theory testing, notes; 'First, there is the logical comparison of the conclusions among themselves, by which the internal consistency of the system is tested.'[3] By implication, failure of this first test signals an end to the testing process and ensures a quick death to the theory.

Cohen and Cyert point out that the empirical testing can only proceed after the logic of the model is proven to be correct: 'The derivation of conclusions of a model from the assumptions is a deductive process in which questions of empirical truth or realism of either assumptions or conclusions are irrelevant. A first test of a model, therefore, is logical consistency.'[4]

The importance of consistency is also manifested in choosing among alternative theories. The standard view of theory selection includes consistency as a major element in evaluating a given theory: 'Disconfirmed, illogical, and cumbersome theories are rejected or reworked; highly confirmed, mutually consistent, fruitful and elegant structures are retained.'[5]

Even Milton Friedman, champion of empirical testing as the sole criterion for theory choice, recognizes a place for consistency. When choosing among theories with equal predictive power and accuracy, 'logical completeness and consistency' can be used as a 'subsidiary' choice rule.[6]

In economics, the importance of consistency is enhanced by the difficulties inherent in empirical testing. In the history of economic thought, the charge of 'inconsistency' has been a powerful means of discrediting rival theories. If true, such an accusation is often enough to destroy a theory.

For instance, note the tremendous research and effort, over a period of almost a century, devoted to solving the 'great contradiction' in Marxist theory; that is, a constant rate of profit and a varying organic composition of capital implies (in direct contradiction to an earlier claim) a varying rate of surplus value. The 'transformation problem' was discussed as if the entire Marxist theorist structure depended on its solution – yielding a consistent theory.[7]

For the modern theory of the firm, consistency is one of the main reasons for its long life. The modern theory of the firm does not survive on the basis of empirical strength. In fact, 'the theory is as frequently contradicted as confirmed by casual evidence'.[8] Its tenacity lies in the internal consistency of the theory – the perfectly interlocking structure of the isoquant, output, and factor market characterizations. The orthodox defense rests not only on the fact that the theory generates testable predictions that have been corroborated, but also that 'the theory is simple, elegant, [and] internally consistent'.[9] Once the theory was synthesized into a consistent whole, individual pieces could not be rejected without throwing out the entire structure.

This section is designed to review what must seem obvious: consistency is a required element of any theory. Instrumentalists, empiricists, Popperians, Lakatosians – all agree that a theory must be internally consistent for it to have any claim as a guide to our understanding of reality. Before the arguments over proper methodology begin, direct contradiction or inconsistency must be removed from a theoretical system. Inconsistency is a black mark that cannot be overcome. For any theory, internal consistency is a crucial, indispensable attribute.

Consistency in the modern theory of the firm

The modern orthodox theory of production and distribution has been basically intact for a half-century. It is composed, as we have seen, of three interlocking optimization problems. The goal of this section is to highlight the most appealing feature of the theory, its consistency.

Consistency is defined as the integration of various pieces into a coherent, systematic whole. Consistency is characterized by the absence of contradiction or opposing results. In general, it is the property of interrelatedness between the pieces of a complicated explanation.

The modern theory of the firm can be divided several different ways. The key point is that the various pieces fit nicely together to form the modern theory of the firm. In this chapter, we will analyze the various subgroups that form the overall theory, constantly stressing the consistent manner in which the pieces fit together.

The main division in the modern theory of the firm is that between the production and distribution sides. The former focuses on optimal rates of output and input usages; the latter examines the distribution of product among the factors of production.

On the production side, the firm can be analyzed from three viewpoints, that is, three different optimization problems. These three facets, consistently interrelated, form the orthodox theory of production. On the distribution side, the theory focuses on one particular optimization problem, using it to explain factor shares and profit. The distribution side also has the property of internal consistency.

The two main sides of the theory of the firm are tied together to form the orthodox theory of production and distribution – what we have called the modern theory of the firm. But the orthodox model does not end there; by synthesizing the theory of the firm (the supply side) with the theory of consumer behaviour (the demand side), the orthodox theory of value is formed.

Neoclassical analysis at every stage is a perfectly consistent, mechanistic model. Given various assumptions and objectives, decisions are made and variables are chosen. Typically, we can examine a decision from several perspectives and, because of the consistent nature of the theory, we are assured of always finding the same result. This is a powerful and appealing property, one that must be maintained if the theory is to survive.

The production side

This section is designed to show explicitly the consistency inherent in the production side of the modern theory of the firm. As we have seen in Chapter 3, the production side is composed of three optimization problems – the isoquant, output, and factor market sides – that interlock to form the modern theory of the firm.

Given a production function, output demand, and input supply functions, and behavioral assumptions (typically, cost minimization and profit maximization), the firm proceeds to determine its optimal choices. The isoquant, output, and factor market sides yield the same results (the same optimal endogenous variable levels), but through different paths. On the isoquant side, the firm chooses the amount of factor use, minimizing the cost of producing a given level of output. The output analysis has the firm choose output such that profit (revenue minus cost) is maximized. Finally, the firm chooses the rate of input use that maximizes profit when solving its factor market optimization problem.

The crucial point is that these different views of the firm's optimization problem will yield equivalent results; this is consistency. Understanding the three facets of the modern theory of the firm is a first step. The next level of comprehension is the awareness of the interrelationships between these different characterizations of the firm's objectives.

The associations binding the three facets are neither haphazard nor indeterminate, but constantly interrelated. A simple graphical juxtaposition of the three characterizations facilitates an intuitive understanding of consistency (Figure 5.1)

Given that the firm wants to produce q^* units of output, the minimum cost combination of inputs is x_i^*, x_j^*. On the factor market side, the profit-maximising rate of input usage is identical (x_i^*, x_j^*). The use of x_i^* and x_j^* units will yield q^* units of output – the profit-maximizing rate of output.

Mathematically, the optimal choices can be compared by analyzing the three optimization problems:

$$\min C(\underline{x}) = \underline{w}'\underline{x} \qquad [1]$$
$$\text{s.t. } \bar{q} = f(\underline{x})$$

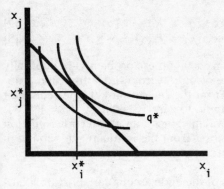

The Isoquant Side

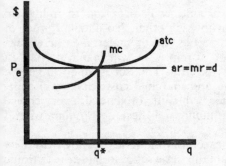

The Output Side

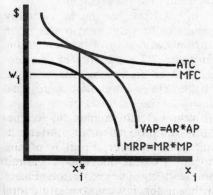

The Factor Market Side

Figure 5.1 Consistency within the modern theory of the firm

$$\max \pi(q) = Pq - C(q) \qquad [2]$$
$$\max \pi(\underline{x}) = Pf(\underline{x}) - \underline{w}'\underline{x} \qquad [3]$$

The solutions derived from each of these problems are internally consistent. The optimal rate of output from the output side (equation [2] is $q^* = h(P,\underline{w})$. From the factor market side (equation [3], the optimal level of inputs to hire is given by $\underline{x}^* = \underline{i}(P,\underline{w})$. Clearly, the two are equivalent since the production function shows $f(\underline{x}^*) = q^*$. Furthermore, from the isoquant side (equation [1]), the cost-minimizing rate of input use, given output level q^*, is $\underline{x}^* = \underline{j}(\underline{w},q^*)$.

Clearly, the optimal rates of the endogenous variables are identical. The firm can choose its optimum values from any three optimization problems and always be assured of internally consistent results.

Changes in exogenous variables will also lead to individual results that are consistent with each other. No detailed proof of these comparative static properties will be undertaken here, but, intuitively, a change in, for example, w_i will manifest itself in every facet of the theory of the firm. The isocost line will have a different slope, the average and marginal cost curves will shift, and the input supply function will shift. In general, every choice variable will have a new optimum and these new optima will all be internally consistent.

The consistency properties of the modern theory of the firm enabled Shephard to generate the same set of testable predictions, or comparative static results, with a completely different and much easier procedure. Instead of the traditional Hicks-Samuelson, constrained Lagrangean method of analysis, the modern duality approach leads to identical results from a different route. Thus the truly 'high-powered', mathematical theory of the firm today uses Shephard's Lemma and Hotelling's Lemma to generate testable predictions from cost functions or profit functions – relying on the fact that the theory of the firm is a web of optimization problems consistently interrelated.

This section was designed to review briefly a main subdivision of the modern theory of the firm – the production side. Attention was focused exclusively on the consistency properties of the theory. Understanding that the production side can be viewed from three distinct angles (isoquant, output, and factor market sides) is important, but the key lies in the consistent interrelationships between these different viewpoints. Thus isoquants, cost curves, and value of marginal product schedules are all intertwined. Whether graphically or mathematically, consistency can be seen by the equivalent results of the different viewpoints. Further, consistency guarantees that exogenous changes must be manifested in the endogenous variables in a consistent fashion, regardless of the viewpoint adopted by the analyst. Finally, this consistency enabled the modern duality approach to develop alternative routes to the same results.

The distribution side

This section reviews the orthodox theory of distribution and its consistency properties. Distribution in orthodox economics can be best understood by analyzing the factor market side of the theory of the firm. Distribution theory in orthodox economics is nothing more than a determination of factor shares, a natural byproduct of the factor market side optimization solution.

On the factor market side (equation 3), the firm chooses the factor combination that maximizes profits. Mathematically, solving the first-order conditions for a maximum for x^*,

$$Pf_i(x) = w_i \qquad\qquad i = 1, \ldots, n$$

yields optimal factor uses that are a function of output and input prices,

$$x^* = g(P, w).$$

Distribution then proceeds simply: each factor is awarded a share equivalent to its input price times its optimal use:

$$\text{Factor } x_i\text{'s share} = w_i x_i^*$$

Fig 5.2 shows that each factor is awarded a return equal to the shaded area; it also shows why the orthodox theory of distribution is also known as the marginal productivity theory of distribution. Clearly, a main determinant of x_i's share is $f_i(x)$ – its marginal product.

It is important to note that in modern microeconomic theory, every productive factor has its own market. Explicit and implicit factors of production have supply and demand curves which give their corresponding input prices. Thus factors provided internally by the firm are rewarded on the same basis as explicit factors.

In a long-run competitive equilibrium, free factor mobility ensures that no non-zero profit situations exist. Thus total revenue will be exactly distributed among all factors, explicit and implicit, according to input price times optimal factor use, $Pq^* = \underline{w}'\underline{x}^*$.

Orthodox profit theory (assuming free entry and exit) makes its

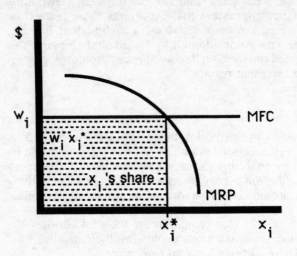

Figure 5.2 The return to a factor

entrance under short-run conditions. In the short run, the variable factors are remunerated as above. The fixed factors, which by definition cannot be varied, simply receive their input price times the fixed factor amount ($\underline{w}'\bar{\underline{x}}$).

It is the presence of fixed factors that allows for the possibility of non-zero profit, that is, total revenue greater or less than the sum of the factor payments:

$$Pq^* \begin{array}{l} \geq \underline{w}'\underline{x}^* \\ < \underline{w}'\bar{\underline{x}}. \end{array} \quad +$$

Figure 5.3 shows an excess profits case. Known as the 'adding up' or 'product exhaustion' problem, the possibility of non-zero profit was seen as problematical by early neoclassical economists. The modern theory of the firm, however, simply posits a residual claimant – the owner of the firm – as the profit receiver.

Importantly, the owner does absolutely nothing for this residual share. In his role as owner he is neither a factor of production, nor optimizing agent, nor uncertainty-bearer. Profit is a pure residual, not a functional return. In orthodox microeconomic theory, profit arises solely from short-run time constraints. Factor fixity is the only cause of a surplus or deficit when comparing total revenue and factor payments. The residual (profit) or shortfall (loss) is not the result of an economic function.

Historically, economics has applied a rather confusing

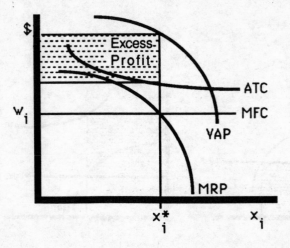

Figure 5.3 Profit on the factor market side

terminology to the study of profit, and modern microeconomic theory is no exception. Perhaps the poorest use of the word centers around 'normal profit'. Given our cost definitions, however, we can see clearly the idea behind this term. Normal profit is not profit in the sense of a residual, but simply the return to the implicit factors. Often these factors are valued according to opportunity cost criteria. Thus normal profit is the next most remunerative income available to the internally provided factors of production.

Economic or excess profit is the true profit term in orthodox theory. Economic profits are the surplus remaining after all factors are remunerated – the explicit factors receiving explicit payments and the implicit factors receiving normal profits. Once again, this residual goes to the owner who does nothing in this capacity; economic, or pure, profit in modern microeconomic theory is a pure residual.

On the production side, consistency was manifested in the interrelations between the three facets of the firm. Consistency properties of the modern theory of the firm are also in evidence on the distribution side. In fact, there are two levels of consistency: within the factor market side and between the output and factor market characterizations.

Orthodox distribution theory is derived from solving the factor

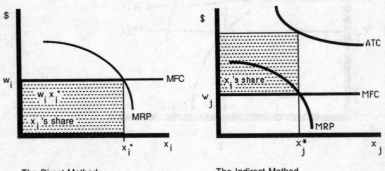

The Direct Method   The Indirect Method

Figure 5.4   Consistency within distribution theory

market side optimization problem. Each factor receives a share equal to its input price times its optimal use. We will call this the direct method of determining distributive shares. The indirect method, on the other hand, determines shares by a residual calculation.

Consistency within the factor market side means that these two methods of determining shares are equivalent. For example, given a two-input production function, input prices and the profit-maximization behavioral assumption, the firm's optimal choices and resulting shares are given by Figure 5.4.

We can calculate x_1's share directly by finding its optimal level of use and multiplying it by the given input price $w_1 x_1^*$ (the direct method) Or we can calculate x_1's share indirectly. After finding x_2's share $(w_2 x_2^*)$, x_1's return per unit of x_2 is any difference between the average total cost (appropriately defined) and the marginal revenue product of x_2. Thus, x_1's share is $(ATC - MRP)x_2^*$ (the indirect method).

The theory guarantees that these two alternative methods of calculating distributive shares will be exactly equivalent. This was Philip Wicksteed's main argument in espousing the marginal pro-

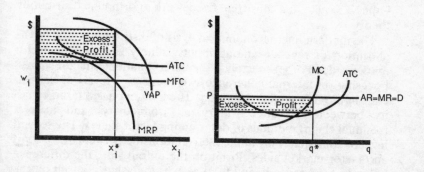

Figure 5.5   Consistency in profit theory

ductivity theory.[10] He argued that the classical economists used several theories to explain distribution, when only one fundamental principle was needed. Consistency was found in the equivalent shares given by the direct (or marginal productivity) and indirect (or residual) methods. No special theory of rent was needed. Rent as a residual equalled the return to land according to marginal productivity.

The second level of consistency on the distribution side is manifested in the interrelationship between the output and factor market derivations of profit. These two alternative determinations of profit are identical. Figure 5.5 shows the output and the factor market graphical expositions. On the output side, profit is total revenue minus total cost (including implicit costs, that is, normal profit). On the factor market side, profit is total revenue product minus total factor cost.

Consistency lies in the fact that these two profit derivations are equivalent. At the optimal levels of outputs and inputs, $(AR - ATC)q^*$ equals $(VAP - ATC)x_i^*$.

The confusing terminology of modern microeconomic profit theory may result in misunderstanding. But it is clear that its theoretical core is consistent. The 'normal profit' contained in the average cost function is reflected in payments to implicit factors

129

on the factor market side. Calculation of the costs according to next-best alternative considerations changes nothing.

Any residual on the factor market side is a true profit, an unimputable surplus. This residual will be reflected on the output side as a difference between total revenue and total cost. Most importantly, these two methods of calculating profit are equivalent – thus revealing the consistent framework of orthodox distribution theory.

The modern microeconomic analysis of distribution, that is, the allocation of revenue among inputs, simply borrows the factor market side in order to explain the determination of factor shares. Focusing on internal coherence, we found two levels of consistency in the theory of distribution. The first emphasized the equality between the direct (marginal productivity) and indirect (residual claim) methods of determining factor shares. The second level of consistency lay in the interrelationship between the output and factor market sides. Profit on the output side, the difference between total revenue and total cost, is the same as profit on the factor market side, the difference between total revenue product and total factor cost. Finally, we found that, in spite of some rather confusing terminology, standard profit theory is also consistent. Every productive factor, explicit and implicit, receives a return according to marginal productivity considerations. The implicit factors' return is termed 'normal profit'. This, however, is not a true profit, but a wage payment. The only true profit, in the sense of an unimputable residual, is due solely to short-run constraints. In this case, factor mobility is impeded and a surplus or deficit may arise. This non-zero residual accrues to the owner who does nothing in his capacity as owner to gain the surplus or bear the loss. Thus orthodox profit theory achieves perfect closure.

This section focused specifically on the internally consistent properties of the modern theory of the firm. The reader should now have an appreciation for the logical cohesiveness of the orthodox theory of production, cost, and distribution. On the production side, the three facets are mutually compatible and reinforcing. On the distribution side, a consistent theory of factor shares and profit can be derived. Together, these two main divisions form the modern theory of the firm.

However, the interrelatedness does not stop within the theory of the firm. The modern theory of the firm is a fundamental part of the orthodox theory of value. Most importantly, in microeconomic theory, interrelatedness exists everywhere, both

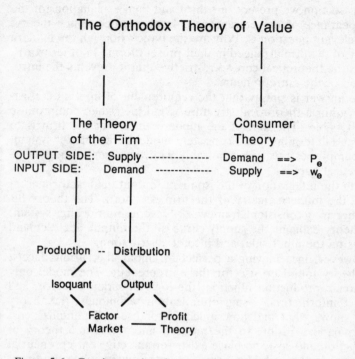

The Orthodox Theory of Value

The Theory of the Firm	Consumer Theory
OUTPUT SIDE: Supply --------------	Demand ==> P_e
INPUT SIDE: Demand --------------	Supply ==> w_e

Production -- Distribution

Isoquant — Output

Factor Market — Profit Theory

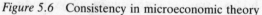

Figure 5.6 Consistency in microeconomic theory

internally and externally. The overall scheme of orthodox micro-economic analysis might look something like Figure 5.6. The theory of the firm provides half of the orthodox scheme – the supply curves in the output markets and demand curves in the input markets. The output demand curves and labor supply curves are provided by consumers, the other half, who maximize utility subject to budget constraints. Thus all prices are determined by demand and supply curves that are, in turn, derived from the application of the logic of rational choice by producers and consumers.

Internally, the various facets fit together perfectly. Externally, in conjunction with consumer theory, the theory of value is neatly organized. That the pieces of the puzzle link smoothly into a unified whole is a very appealing attribute and one that, we will argue, must be maintained if the theory is to survive.

The third level of explanation – consistency over entrepreneurship

In this section we present our third and final explanation for the disappearance of the entrepreneur from microeconomic theory. The relevant question is: Why are the basic axioms in the modern theory of the firm arranged in their present form? In other words, why is the theoretical core so restrictive that it prevents the introduction of the entrepreneur?

The answer is simply that the requirement of internal consistency within a theoretical structure is indispensable, compromise is impossible. The aim of the modern theory of the firm is to present a determinate and consistent model of the market system. It accomplishes this task admirably with the essential help of its theoretical core.

With the integration of the isoquant, output, and factor market sides, the modern theory of the firm was born. The theory fits together in a consistent framework. In one interlocking system, the theory explains the supply curve on the output side, demand curves on the input side, and income distribution.

However, in achieving a perfect fit among the various facets, the theory found no use for the entrepreneur. The model only requires a production function, the logic of rational choice, and perfect information. Using optimization techniques, the theory itself shows what and how much factor use will minimize cost and maximize profit. In the modern microeconomic theory of production and cost, no place exists for an active entrepreneurial function. In the orthodox firm, the entrepreneur plays an essentially sterile role, choosing the optimum values of the endogenous variables.

Significantly, not only is entrepreneurship unnecessary, but it threatens the interlocking structure that is the hallmark of the modern theory of the firm. Thus it is not a question of redundancy, but one of mutual exclusivity; the entrepreneur and consistency cannot co-exist.

Why can't the entrepreneur as innovator be incorporated into the modern theory of the firm? Because the production function exactly describes every possible input-output relationship; because the logic of rational choice requires that the ends and means be known and given. The introduction of innovation requires relaxing these core assumptions, but this, in turn, is impossible; the consistent, interlocking nature of the theory would be destroyed.

Why can't the entrepreneur as uncertainty-bearer be incorporated into the modern theory of the firm? Because perfect information, a fundamental assumption, guarantees every agent's expectations will be exactly fulfilled. The introduction of uncertainty requires relaxing this assumption, but this, in turn, would prevent the application of the logic of rational choice. Decision-making would now have some real meaning, but the resulting destruction of the consistent framework of the theory is unacceptable.

Why can't the entrepreneur as coordinator be incorporated into the modern theory of the firm? Because perfect information and the logic of rational choice exactly determine the only viable alternative. True coordination requires relaxing these assumptions, but the immediate consequence, the breakdown of the model, is too costly.

Why can't the entrepreneur as arbitrageur be incorporated into the modern theory of the firm? Because perfect information prevents the introduction of ignorance, a requirement for arbitrage. Once again, relaxing this assumption in order to allow arbitrage has too high a cost – the removal of a crucial attribute, consistency, from the theory.

In every case, the entrepreneur is prevented from playing a role by the modern theory of the firm's theoretical core. The three basic axioms are arranged the way they are so as to guarantee an internally consistent framework. This is one of the most appealing features of the model and a basic defense against attack. When the pieces of the firm were integrated, consistency was recognized as the key attribute. The perfect fit could not be disturbed. Any attempt at the introduction of an entrepreneurial role causes inconsistency. And, in general, inconsistency is a charge from which it is impossible to recover. For this reason, the entrepreneur was elevated to a meaningless role, that of optimizing agent.

In fact, the human element, in general, is of no consequence in modern orthodox theory. Georgescu-Roegen explicitly points to the 'special pride' economists take in creating a consistent, interlocking system:

> Standard economics takes special pride in operating with a man-less picture. As Pareto overtly claimed, once we have determined the means at the disposal of the individual and obtained a 'photograph of his tastes . . . the individual may disappear'. The individual is thus reduced to a mere subscript in the ophelimity function $\phi_i(X)$. The logic is perfect: man is not an economic agent simply because there is no economic process. There is only a jigsaw puzzle of fitting given means to given ends, which requires a computer not an agent.[11]

The modern theory of the firm is entirely self-contained; it is a perfectly consistent system, given its assumptions. The presentation of the theory by its founders focused on this powerful and attractive property.

Samuelson, for example, clearly understood the crucial attribute of interrelatedness. He believed logical coherence to be an important element and one that should be explicitly presented:

> Economic theory as taught in the textbooks has often tended to become segmentalized into loosely integrated compartments, such as production, value, and distribution. There are, no doubt, pedagogical advantages in such a treatment and yet something of the *essential unity and interdependence* of economic forces is lost in so doing. A case in point is the conventional assuming of a cost curve for each firm and the working out of its optimum output with respect to its demand conditions. Only later is the problem of the purchase of factors of production by the firm investigated, and often its connection with the previous process is not brought out.[12]

Samuelson rails against those who assume linearly homogenous production functions and non-constant average and marginal cost curves: 'It is indicative of the lack of integration mentioned above that many writers assume U-shaped cost curves in the same breath with homogeneity of the product function.'[13]

Carlson, whose *Study on the Pure Theory of Production* is essentially his doctoral dissertation at the University of Chicago, is also very aware of the advantage a theory has when it can claim a harmonious interrelationship among its constituent parts:

> Although economists have long recognized the main relationships of the theory of production, these relationships have not been co-ordinated in a single body of theory – except in such works as those of Frisch and Schneider – but have been scattered in isolated fragments throughout cost theory, capital and interest theory and the theory of distribution. To bring together and co-ordinate in one *consistent* scheme the different relationships of the theory of production has been the main purpose of this essay.[14]

Frisch applauds the 'classical' (i.e., orthodox) methodology, which emphasizes the

> fundamental logic of the laws of production . . . I have retained my admiration for the classical ideas also after I started to devote a good part of my time and energy to

mathematical programming. I have felt it a mission to safeguard the classical ideas, to systematize and develop them, and to endeavour to present the whole in a coherent and logical form.[15]

And this he certainly does. Frisch repeatedly highlights the interrelationships inherent in the theory and the fact that equivalent results are reached independent of the manner in which the problem is formulated.

Above we have discussed profit-maximization adjustment in two stages. First we discussed substitution adjustment [the isoquant side], and found b [total cost] as a function of x [quantity] along the substitumal [the least-cost expansion path or cost function], we then discussed volume adjustment (scale adjustment) by finding the point on the substitumal where the difference between total income and variable costs was greatest [the output side]. Profit-maximization adjustment can, however, also be discussed directly in one stage, that is to say, without going via the substitumal. This is done by determining the quantities of the variable factors, $v_1, \ldots v_n$, which make

$$r = Px(v_1, \ldots v_n) - \Sigma \, q_i \, v_i$$

as large as possible [the factor market side] . . . [16]
    For certain questions the direct method is the simplest, but the argument via the substitumal gives a better understanding of several questions.[17]

There is no doubt that the founders of the modern theory of the firm were aware of the powerful property of consistency. As an integrated whole, the modern theory of the firm presents a logically perfect, self-contained explanation of production, cost, and distribution. In conjunction with the theory of consumer behavior, the orthodox theory of value is, similarly, a consistent, deterministic system. Nothing can disturb this perfect system, not even the entrepreneur, for the entire structure comes and goes as one. Pieces cannot be broken off, reorganized, and then reinserted. If a change is to be made, the whole structure must be torn down and then rebuilt. It is this tight, interlocking attribute which, initially, made the theory so appealing and which, today, accounts for its resistance to change. Improvement can be made in one of the nested sub-groups of the overall theory, but the cost of tearing down the rest of the edifice is what makes any such change problematic.

Conclusion

This chapter presented our third level of explanation for the disappearance of the entrepreneur from modern microeconomic theory. The key, of course, lies in consistency.

In the first section, we argued that consistency is a fundamental test any theory must pass in order to gain serious consideration. Common sense alone dictates that a theoretical structure which includes internally contradictory statements or results cannot convey absolute truth. Economic theories, because of the difficulty of empirical testing, especially depend on such criteria as elegance, simplicity, and, perhaps most importantly, internal consistency.

In the second section, we showed the consistent properties inherent in the modern theory of the firm. On the production side, consistency manifested itself in several different ways: (1) equivalent results can be obtained through the isoquant, output, or factor market solutions; (2) exogenous shocks lead to the same results independent of the optimization problem being analyzed; and, finally, (3) the traditional analysis of Hicks-Samuelson-Allen *et al.* can be done more quickly and easily using the modern duality approach. On the distribution side, consistency means that factor shares are equivalent when derived by alternative means and that profit can be shown by either the output or the factor market side. Finally, we saw how, the theory of the firm as a whole can be integrated with consumer theory to form the orthodox theory of value.

We then had the means to show the motivation behind the exclusion of the entrepreneur from modern neoclassical theory. In our second level of explanation, we argued the entrepreneur is unable to occupy a place in the theory of the firm because of the postulates found in the theoretical core. The model is a mechanical abstraction and totally self-contained, it automatically reaches an equilibrium position, given its constraints. The important point is not that marginalism or mathematical techniques used for such concepts had been introduced over a half-century before the exit of the entrepreneur from orthodox microeconomic theory. Early and mature neoclassical theories are testimony to the ability of the entrepreneur to survive in a mathematical environment. The key lies in the tightly interlocking nature of the theory of the firm. It was when the three facets of the theory were synthesized, during the modern microeconomic era, that the entrepreneur disappeared.

On a deeper level, the third level of explanation, we argued that it is the consistent properties of the model that prevent entrepreneurial considerations from being allowed to play a role. The theory is not accepted merely because it is a mechanical model; it has not enjoyed such a long life because it is deterministic. A wide variety of attacks batter the theory, but cannot bring it down. That there is no better alternative is obviously important, but that the pieces cohere perfectly is no less crucial to its continued survival. The introduction of the entrepreneur would destroy this key attribute; for this reason, and this reason alone, the entrepreneur disappeared and has been unable to play a meaningful role in the modern theory of the firm. We argued, therefore, that the motivation behind the exclusion of the entrepreneur from microeconomic theory is to allow the consistent, self-contained model to operate unhindered. The entrepreneur is shorthand for uncertainty, imperfect information, and the unknown. He operates in the shadowy world of intuition, ignorance, and disequilibrium. As a functional agent, he is completely outside the scope of modern orthodox economic analysis because entrepreneurial issues are irrelevant and, more important, inadmissible, in the deterministic, tightly interlocking theoretical environment that is modern microeconomic theory. The entrepreneur cannot be introduced into the modern theory of the firm because he directly clashes with consistency – this is a battle the entrepreneur has not won.

Notes

1 Bruce J. Caldwell, *Beyond Positivism: Economic Methodology in the Twentieth Century* (London: George Allen & Unwin, 1982), p. 232.

2 Nicolas Georgescu-Roegan, *Analytical Economics* (Cambridge, Mass.: Harvard University Press, 1967), p. 13.

3 Karl Popper, *The Logic of Scientific Discovery* (New York: Basic Books, 1959), p. 32.

4 Kalman J. Cohen and Richard M. Cyert, *The Theory of the Firm*, 2nd edn (Englewood Cliffs, N.J.: Prentice-Hall, 1975; originally published 1965).

5 Vincent J. Tarascio and Bruce J. Caldwell, 'Theory choice in economics: Philosophy and Practice', *Journal of Economic Issues* 13 December 1979; 984.

6 Milton Friedman, *Essays in Positive Economics* (Chicago: University of Chicago Press, 1953), p. 10.

7 See Mark Blaug, *Economic Theory in Retrospect*, 3rd edn (Cambridge: Cambridge University Press, 1978; originally published 1962), p. 304, for a review of some prominent participants in the debate.

8 Mark Blaug. *The Methodology of Economics: Or How Economists Explain* (Cambridge: Cambridge University Press 1980), p. 177

9 Blaug. *Methodology*, p. 176.

10 Philip Wicksteed, *Essay on the Co-ordination of the Laws of Distribution* London: Macmillan and Co., 1894.

11 Georgescu-Roegen, *Analytical Economics*, p. 104.

12 Paul Samuelson, *Foundations of Economic Analysis* enlarged edition (Cambridge, Mass.: Harvard University Press, 1983; originally published 1947), p. 57 (emphasis added).

13 Samuelson, *Foundations*. p. 85.

14 Sune Carlson, *A Study on the Pure Theory of Production* (London: P. S. King & Son, Ltd., 1939), p.v.

15 Ragnar Frisch, *Theory of Production*, trans. by R. I. Christophersen (Chicago: Rand McNally, 1965; originally published 1935), p. 6.

16 Frisch, *Theory of Production*. 179–80.

17 Frisch, *Theory of Production*, p. 356.

Chapter six

Conclusion

We began by noting, in Chapter 1, the wide variety of fundamental explanatory roles the entrepreneur has played in the history of economic thought. We arranged entrepreneurial functions according to their role in the productive process – a procedure that yielded four basic entrepreneurial functions: coordination, arbitrage, innovation, and uncertainty-bearing.

In order to illustrate the key roles the entrepreneur has played, we tied each function to the theory from which it came. Thus we reviewed coordination as the essential function in Jean-Baptiste Say's classical theory of production and distribution. The entrepreneur as arbitrageur was found to be the driving force in Israel Kirzner's view of the market system. As innovator, the entrepreneur was a key element in Joseph Schumpeter's grand theory of economic development. Finally, the entrepreneur as uncertainty-bearer played fundamental roles in three theories: as speculator for Richard Cantillon, as owner for Frederick Hawley, and as responsible decision-maker for Frank Knight. Thus we demonstrated the wide variety of crucial roles played by the entrepreneur. From Cantillon to Kirzner, theorists have investigated the entrepreneur in their quest to gain insight into the market system.

In Chapter 2, we turned our attention to the entrepreneur in microeconomic theory. Our interest was piqued by the fact that, today, orthodox microeconomic theory makes no use of entrepreneurship in any of its four functional roles. We began, therefore, a review of research into entrepreneurial issues in standard microeconomic theory.

We divided the history of present-day microeconomic theory into three eras. In the first era, the early neoclassical period, the entrepreneur played his usual variety of functional roles. The Lausanne school, focusing on general equilibrium, was able to ignore entrepreneurial considerations because of the nature of the questions being asked. However, in England and the United

States, the entrepreneur reigned as a crucial factor in the neo-classical explanation of the market system. The situation remained unchanged during the mature neoclassical era. Alfred Marshall defined orthodox economics and his focus on the entrepreneur guaranteed continued research into entrepreneurial issues. In addition, this era saw the rise of two great entrepreneurial theories. Joseph Schumpeter's theory of economic development assigned a key role to the entrepreneur as innovator; Frank Knight's entrepreneur as responsible decision-maker, in a world of true uncertainty, was an indispensable element in his theory of production and profit.

Importantly, it was not a particular definition of entrepreneurship that drew our attention, but the fact that debate over the entrepreneur existed. We never presented a particular entrepreneurial theory as the 'right' one; the point was that the entrepreneur played a key explanatory role, for a wide variety of reasons, during the early and mature neoclassical eras.

It was in the third period, the modern microeconomic era, that the situation changed drastically. We found no further research into entrepreneurial issues within orthodox microeconomics. The word 'entrepreneur' was still in use, but it had lost any real meaning. It no longer played a crucial role in the orthodox explanatory scheme.

The obvious question, and one that occupied our attention for the remainder of this work, is: Why did the entrepreneur, a fundamental element throughout the history of economic thought and a key part of early and mature neoclassical economic thought disappear from orthodox microeconomic theory? The next three chapters were devoted to answering this question. We presented three different levels of explanation.

The first level (Chapter 3) was a simple 'eyewitness account' of the disappearance. Certainly the most superficial level of analysis, we observed that the decline of the entrepreneur exactly coincided with the rise of the modern theory of the firm. The proof for our observation lay in a comparison of the history of the entrepreneur and the development of the modern theory of the firm. We clearly saw that the incorporation of the modern theory of the firm into orthodox economics (denoting the beginning of the modern microeconomic era) occurred simultaneous with the disappearance of the entrepreneur from microeconomics.

The natural question of why this happened led to our second level of explanation – a detailed analysis of, or rationale for, the disappearance (Chapter 4). We found that the modern theory of the firm contains three core assumptions (the production function, the logic of rational choice, and perfect information) which effectively bar the introduction of the entrepreneur in any of its varied roles. Since the modern theory of the firm became orthodox microeconomic theory, the entrepreneur was obviously barred from consideration.

Once again, we asked why the core axioms necessarily exclude entrepreneurship. The answer to this question, our third and deepest level of explanation, lies in the desirability of creating a consistent, interlocking theory. In Chapter 5, we showed the indispensable attribute of consistency within a theoretical structure in general and, especially, in economics. We then showed how the modern theory of the firm exactly meets consistency requirements: several pieces (isoquant, output and factor market sides) join to form bigger pieces (the production side) which join with still other pieces (the distribution side) to form the modern theory of the firm. Furthermore, in conjunction with consumer theory, the orthodox theory of value is formed. The whole system, internally and externally, is a perfect set of interlocking relationships. Consistency represents a professional norm reflecting a mechanistic conception of real-world phenomena. The orthodox theory of value is the ultimate fulfillment, in economics, of a perfectly interlocking, self-contained model.

This consistency depends crucially on the three core assumptions. Relaxing these assumptions destroys consistency, but relaxing these assumptions is the only way to include the entrepreneur. Simply put, entrepreneurship is above 'formalization' – it cannot be neatly packaged within a mechanistic, deterministic model. Importantly, the choice is an 'either-or' proposition; there is no happy medium. The corner solution which economic theory has chosen is consistency and for this reason the entrepreneur disappeared from microeconomic theory.

The story is complete, but implications remain. This work has been an exercise, as much as possible, in 'positive' analysis, no value judgments have been made. It is not argued that the entrepreneur should be immediately introduced into economic theory no matter what the cost. We are certainly not prepared to castigate the Hicks-Allen-Samuelson *et al*. group for leading us down the wrong road. We simply posed an interesting problem and presented a possible explanation.

A different issue is the state of present-day, orthodox microeconomic theory. Today, we hear rumblings of discontent within orthodox microeconomic theory. Has modern microeconomics reached a cul-de-sac? Have we finally exhausted the possibility of new developments within the context of the modern theory of the firm? Georgescu-Roegen, writing in 1965, believes we have:

> The task of science is not to climb up the easiest ladder and remain there forever distilling and redistilling the same pure stuff. Standard economics, by opposing any suggestion that the economic process may consist of something more than a jigsaw puzzle with all its elements given, has identified itself with dogmatism.[1]

If this point is true, what is the alternative? By relaxing the core assumptions, especially perfect information, new questions and problems will arise. This will occur, however, only through genuine revolution. We have learned that marginal adjustments toward a new theory are impossible; in this case, it is an all-or-nothing proposition.

It is ironic that the attribute, consistency, which provided the theory one of its greatest advantages and helped its rapid acceptance is now the main obstacle to progress. This is the application of a general rule to a special case: it is much easier to impose change, in a disorganized environment than in an organized environment. Were microeconomics in a state of flux, with many competing views of the world, research into the entrepreneur would certainly be one of the many competitors. However, the current state of microeconomics can be better described as operating in closed, fixed surroundings. Thus, slow, steady improvement in the theory is impossible; the only change possible is radical, discontinuous change. Because of the consistent, intertwined nature of the theory, change in orthodox microeconomics must be revolutionary change.

The theoretical revolution's trigger mechanism will be dissatisfaction with the way that modern microeconomic theory handles technological change. By selecting core postulates that make the problem of static allocation solvable, the modern theory of the firm is setting itself up for a crisis because there are phenomena (not the least of which is dynamic, endogenous change) that it will never be able to explain.

Interestingly, some try to brace the rigorous version of the modern theory of the firm with a set of verbal, anecdotal supports. Thus we see a definite tension between what Kay calls the formal and informal theories of orthodox economics:

> The picture of the brave buccaneering entrepreneur painted by such as the Friedmans [for Kay, the quintessential orthodox economist] in their informal discussions, is curiously

at odds with the limited role afforded to the entrepreneur in formal neoclassical [i.e., orthodox] theory. In the latter, the entrepreneur has no discretion over which actions to take; the choice is made for him by the rules and conditions of the neoclassical game . . . The buccaneer of the Friedman analysis is reduced to an ordinary seaman, with no decision-making capacity, no requirement for initiative, and no discretion over choice of future action. The elimination of ignorance, risk and uncertainty similarly eliminates the need for decision, choice and entrepreneurship as defined by the Friedmans. As Shackle confirms, perfect foresight renders decision-making empty. Again, we find the informal discussion of neoclassical theorists at odds with their formal analysis.[2]

This tension is at the core of current disenchantment with micro-theory. It is clear that technological change is the hallmark of the market system and that economics needs a theoretical framework that allows for research into endogenous, dynamic change of every kind. Intuition, common sense, and the history of economic thought as far back as Cantillon point to the entrepreneur as a key agent in a market economy. Entrepreneurship in any or all of its different roles is essential if we are to understand how the market system generates change and growth.

The modern theory of the firm and the orthodox theory of value cannot tackle this problem through informal theories. And as we have repeatedly seen, it is unable to consider entrepreneurship directly. Modern microeconomics can only take refuge by pointing to its crowning achievement – consistency.

A perfectly consistent, mechanistic model which, by assumption, excludes the entrepreneur and cannot therefore address the issue of technological change must have much in its favor to outweigh this glaring omission. Until now, consistency has played the role of a counterbalance and the modern theory of the firm has survived. Consistency, the perfect interrelatedness of the various pieces in a jigsaw puzzle, won out over entrepreneurship in the first round. But the conflict is not over. The entrepreneur, as we have so often noted, is a crucial actor in the market system. Any attempt to incorporate human elements – imagination, opportunism, or initiative – in an explanation of the market system will immediately focus on entrepreneurial elements.

More and more, however, we see economists introducing 'imperfect information'. As economics moves toward relaxing the core assumptions, toward incorporating 'human elements', and toward explaining technological change, the entrepreneur will reappear. It would be wise, therefore, to review past entrepreneurial theories – using the history of economic and entrepreneurial thought as a guide in avoiding previous mistakes and as an indicator of the most promising available routes.

Notes

1 Nicolas Georgescu-Roegen, *Analytical Economics*: *Issues and Problems* (Cambridge, Mass.: Harvard University Press, 1966), p. 104 (footnote omitted).
2 Neil M. Kay, *The Emergent Firm* (New York: St. Martin's Press, 1984), p. 57 (footnote omitted).

Bibliography

Aitken, Hugh G. J. (ed.) (1965) *Explorations in Enterprise*, Cambridge, Mass.: Harvard University Press.

Alchian, A. A. and Demsetz, H. (1972) 'Production, information costs and economic organization', *American Economic Review* 62: 777–95.

Allen, R. G. D. (1932) 'The foundations of a mathematical theory of exchange', *Economica*, New Series 12; 197–226.

—— (1932) 'Decreasing costs: A mathematical note', *Economic Journal* 42; 323–6.

—— (1933–4) 'The nature of indifference curves', *Review of Economic Studies* 1; 110–21.

—— (1938) *Mathematical Analysis for Economists*, London: Macmillan and Co.

Andrews, P. W. S. (1964) *On Competition in Economic Theory*, London: Macmillan.

Baranzini, Mauro (ed.) (1982) *Advances in Economic Theory*, New York: St. Martin's Press.

Baumol, W. J. (1968) 'Entrepreneurship in economic theory,' *American Economic Review* (Papers and Proceedings) 58; 64–71.

Bell, Daniel and Kristol, Irving (1981) *The Crisis in Economic Theory*, New York: Basic Books.

Bell, John Fred (1967) *A History of Economic Thought*, New York: Ronald Press Co.

Blaug, Mark (1978) *Economic Theory in Retrospect*, 3rd edn, Cambridge: Cambridge University Press.

—— (1980) *The Methodology of Economics*, Cambridge: Cambridge University Press.

Bowley, Arthur L. (1924) *The Mathematical Groundwork of Economics*, Oxford: Clarendon Press.

Brown, E. H. Phelps (1936) *The Framework of the Pricing System*, London: Chapman & Hall.

Buchanon, James M. (1969) *Cost and Choice*, Chicago: Markham Publishing Co.

Buchanon, James M. and Thirlby, George F. (eds.) (1973) *LSE Essays on Cost*, London: Weidenfeld and Nicholson.

Caldwell, Bruce J. (1982) *Beyond Positivism*, London: George Allen and Unwin.

Cantillon Richard (1931) *Essai sur la Nature du Commerce en General*, trans. by Henry Higgs (ed.), London: Macmillan and Co.

Carlson, Sune (1939) *A Study on the Pure Theory of Production*, London: P. S. King & Son.

Casson, Mark (1982) *The Entrepreneur: An Economic Theory*, Totowa, N. J.: Barnes and Noble Books.

Chapman, Sidney J. (1906) 'The remuneration of employers', *Economic Journal* 16; 523–8.

Clark, John Bates (1899) *The Distribution of Wealth*, London: Macmillan.

—— (1922) *Essentials of Economic Theory*, New York: Macmillan.

Clark, J. B. and Giddings, F. H. (1888) *The Modern Distributive Process*, Boston: Ginn and Co.

Clemence, R. V. and Dowdy, F. S. (1950) *The Schumpeterian System*, Cambridge, Mass.: Addison Wesley.

Coase, R. H. (1937) 'The nature of the firm, *Economica*, New Series; 386–405.

—— 1937–8) 'Some notes on monopoly price,' *Review of Economic Studies* 5; 17–31.

Cohen, Kalman J. and Cyert, Richard M. (1975) *The Theory of the Firm*, 2nd edn, Englewood Cliffs, N. J.: Prentice-Hall.

Cournot, Augustin (1929) *Researches into the Mathematical Principles of the Theory of Wealth*, trans. by Nathaniel T. Bacon, New York: Macmillan.

Davenport, Herbert J. (1908) *Value and Distribution*, Chicago: University of Chicago Press.

—— (1913) *Economics of Enterprise*, New York: Macmillan.

Dempsey, Bernard W. (1960) *The Frontier Wage*, Chicago: Loyola University Press.

Dobb, Maurice (1926) *Capitalist Enterprise and Social Progress*, 2nd edn, London: George Routledge & Sons.

—— (1973) *Theories of Value and Distribution Since Adam Smith*, Cambridge: Cambridge University Press.

Doll, John P. and Orazen, Frank (1978) *Production Economics: Theory with Applications*, Columbus: Grid.

Edgeworth, Francis Y. (1925) *Papers Relating to Political Economy* vols. 1–3, London: Macmillan and Co.

—— (1932) *Mathematical Psychics*, London: LSE, Reprints of Scarce Tracts.

Evans, George H., Jr. (1949) 'The entrepreneur and economic theory: A historical and analytical approach', *American Economic Review* (Papers and Proceedings) 39, 336–48.

Ferguson, Charles E. (1969) *The Neoclassical Theory of Production and Distribution*, London: Cambridge University Press.

—— (1972) *Microeconomic Theory*, 3rd edn., Homewood, Ill.: Richard D. Irwin.

Fetter, Frank A. (1918) *Economic Principles*, New York: Century Co.

Finkel, Sidney R. and Tarascio, Vincent J. (1971) *Wage and Employment Theory*, New York: Ronald Press Company.

Fisher, Irving (1910) *Elementary Principles of Economics*, New York: Macmillan.

—— (1925) *Mathematical Investigations in the Theory of Value and Prices*, New Haven: Yale University Press.

Flux, A. W. (1894) 'A review of Wicksteed's *Co-ordination*', *Economic Journal* 4; 308–13.

Fraser, Lindley M. (1937) *Economic Thought and Language*, London: A & C Black Ltd.

Friedman, Milton (1953) *Essays in Positive Economics*, Chicago: University of Chicago Press.

—— (1962) *Price Theory*, New York: Aldine Publishing Co.

Frisch, Ragnar (1965) *Theory of Production*, trans. by R. I. Christophersen, Chicago: Rand McNally.

Fusfeld, Daniel R. (1980) 'The conceptual framework of modern economics', *Journal of Economic Issues* 14; 1–52.

Georgescu-Roegen, Nicholas (1966) *Analytical Economics: Issues and Problems*, Cambridge, Mass.: Harvard University Press.

Haney, Lewis H. (1949) *History of Economic Thought*, New York: Macmillan Co.

Harrod, Roy F. (1930) 'Notes on supply', *Economic Journal* 40; 232–41.

—— (1934) 'Doctrines of imperfect competition', *Quarterly Journal of Economics* 48; 442–70.

Haveman, Robert H. and Knopf Kenyon A. (1966) *The Market System*, New York: John Wiley and Sons.

Hawley, Frederick B. (1893) 'The risk theory of profit', *Quarterly Journal of Economics* 7; 459–79.

—— (1900) 'Enterprise and profit', *Quarterly Journal of Economics* 15; 75–105.

—— (1907) *Enterprise and the Productive Process*, New York: G. P. Putnam's Sons.

—— (1927) 'The orientation of economics on enterprise', *American Economic Review* 17; 409–28.

Hebert, Robert F. and Link, Albert. (1982) *The Entrepreneur: Mainstream Views and Radical Critiques*, New York: Praeger.

Henderson, James M and Quandt, Richard E. (1980) *Microeconomic Theory: A Mathematical Approach*, 3rd edn, New York: McGraw Hill.

Hess, James D. (1983) *The Economics of Organization*, Amsterdam: North-Holland.

Hicks, John R. (1931) 'The theory of uncertainty and profit', *Economica*, New Series 11; 170–89.

—— (1932) 'Marginal productivity and the principle of variation', *Economica*, New Series 12; 79–88.

—— (1932) 'A reply,' *Economica*, New Series 12; 297–300.

—— (1963) *The Theory of Wages*, 2nd edn, London: Macmillan.

—— (1983) *Value and Capital* 2nd edn, Oxford: Clarendon Press.

Hicks, John R. and Allen, R. G. D. (1934) 'A reconsideration of the theory of value', Part 1, *Economica*, New Series 1; 52–76.
—— (1934) 'A reconsideration of the theory of value', Part 2, *Economica*, New Series 1; 196–219.
Hopkins, William S. 'Profit in American economic theory', *Review of Economic Studies* 1; 60–66.
Hunt, E. K. (1979) *History of Economic Thought: A Critical Perspective*, Belmont, Ca.: Wadsworth Publishing Co.
Johnson, W. E. (1913) 'The pure theory of utility curves', *Economic Journal* 23; 483–513.
Kaldor, Nicholas (1934) 'The equilibrium of the firm', *Economic Journal* 44; 60–76.
—— (1935) 'Market imperfections and excess capacity', *Economica*, New Series 2; 33–50.
—— (1955–6) 'Alternative theories of distribution', *Review of Economic Studies* 23; 83–100.
—— (1966) 'Marginal productivity and the macro-economic theories of distribution', *Review of Economic Studies* 33; 309–19.
—— (1980) *Essays on Value and Distribution*, 2nd edn, New York: Holmes and Meier Publishers.
Kay, Neil M. (1984) *The Emergent Firm*, New York: St. Martin's Press.
Keynes, John Maynard (1936) *The General Theory of Employment, Interest and Money*, New York: Harcourt, Brace and Co.
Kirzner, Israel M. (1973) *Competition and Entrepreneurship*, Chicago: University of Chicago Press.
—— (1979) *Perception, Opportunity and Profit*, Chicago: University of Chicago Press.
—— (1980) 'The primacy of entrepreneurial discovery', in I. M. Kirzner (ed.) *The Prime Mover of Progress: The Entrepreneur in Capitalism and Socialism*, London: Institute of Economic Affairs.
—— (1985) *Discovery and the Capitalist Process*, Chicago: University of Chicago Press.
Knight, Frank H. (1921) *Risk, Uncertainty and Profit*, New York: Houghton Mifflin Co.
—— (1925) 'A note on Professor Clark's illustration of marginal productivity', *Journal of Political Economy* 33; 550–53.
—— (1933) *The Economic Organization*, Chicago: University of Chicago Press.
—— (1934) 'The common sense of political economy (Wicksteed reprinted)', *Journal of Political Economy* 42; 660–73.
Koolman, George (1971) 'Say's conception of the role of the entrepreneur', *Economica*, New Series 38; 269–86.
Kuenne, Robert E. (1968) *Microeconomic Theory of the Market Mechanism*, New York: Macmillan.
Lamberton, Dennis M. (1965) *The Theory of Profit*, Oxford: Blackwell and Mott.
Lehfeldt, R. A. (1925) 'Analysis of profit', *Journal of Political Economy* 33; 278–92.

Leibenstein, Harvey (1966) 'Allocative efficiency vs. "X-efficiency" ' *American Economic Review* 56; 392–415.

────── (1976) *Beyond Economic Man*, Cambridge, Mass.: Harvard University Press.

Leontief, Wassily (1934) 'Interest on capital and distribution: A problem in the theory of marginal productivity', *Quarterly Journal of Economics* 49; 147–61.

Lewis, Ben W. (1937) 'The corporate entrepreneur', *Quarterly Journal of Economics* 51; 535–44.

Liebhafsky, H. H. (1963) *The Nature of Price Theory*, Homewood, Ill.: Dorsey Press.

MacDougall, G. D. A. (1936) 'The definition of prime and supplementary costs', *Economic Journal* 46; 443–61.

Machlup, Fritz (1978) *Methodology of Economics and Other Social Sciences*, New York: Academic Press.

Marris, Robin (1964) *The Economic Theory of 'Managerial' Capitalism*, New York: The Free Press of Glencoe.

────── (1972) 'Why economics needs a theory of the firm', *Economic Journal* 82 (supplement); 321–52.

Marshall, Alfred (1961) *Principles of Economics* 9th (Variorum) edn, annotations by C. W. Guillebaud, New York: Macmillan.

Matyas, Antal (1980) *History of Modern Non-Marxian Economics*, Budapest: Akademiai Kiado.

Mill, John Stuart (1909) *Principles of Political Economy*, W. J. Ashley (ed.), London: Longmans.

Mises, Ludwig von (1949) *Human Action*, London: William Hodge.

Moore, Henry L. (1925) 'A moving equilibrium of demand and supply', *Quarterly Journal of Economics* 39; 357–71.

────── (1929) *Synthetic Economics* New York: Macmillan.

Nell, E. J. (1980) 'Capital and the firm in neoclassical theory', *Journal of Post Keynesian Economics* 2; 494–508.

Obrinsky, Mark (1983) *Profit Theory and Capitalism*, Philadelphia: University of Pennsylvania Press.

Pareto, Vilfredo (1971) *Manual of Political Economy*, trans. by Ann Schwier, Ann Schwier and Alfred Page (eds), New York: Augustus M. Kelley.

Pasinetti, Luigi (1977) *Lectures on the Theory of Production*, New York: Columbia University Press.

Pettengill, Robert B. (1947) *Price Economics*, New York: Ronald Press Co.

Pibram, Karl (1983) *A History of Economic Reasoning*, Baltimore: Johns Hopkins University Press.

Pigou, A. C. (1920) *Economics of Welfare*, London: Macmillan and Co.

────── (1927) 'The laws of diminishing and increasing cost', *Economic Journal* 37; 188–97.

Popper, Karl (1959) *The Logic of Scientific Discovery*, New York: Basic Books.

149

Redlich, F. (1949) 'The origin of the concepts of "Entrepreneur" and "Creative Entrepreneur" ', *Explorations in Entrepreneurial History* 1 (1); 1–7.

Robbins, Lionel (1928) 'The representative firm', *Economic Journal* 38; 387–404.

––––– (1962) *An Essay on the Nature and Significance of Economic Science*, London: Macmillan.

Robinson, E. A. G. (1934) 'The problem of management and the size of firms', *Economic Journal* 44; 240–54.

Robinson, Joan (1932) 'Imperfect competition and falling supply price', *Economic Journal* 42; 544–54.

––––– (1934) 'Euler's theorem and the problem of distribution', *Economic Journal* 44; 398–414.

––––– (1934) 'What is perfect competition?' *Quarterly Journal of Economics* 49; 104–20.

––––– (1969) *The Economics of Imperfect Competition*, 2nd edn, London: Macmillan.

Roll, Eric (1974) *A History of Economic Thought*, 4th edn, Homewood, Ill.: Richard D. Irwin.

Ryan, W. L. (1958) *Price Theory*, London: Macmillan & Co.

Samuelson, Paul A. (1938) 'A note on the pure theory of consumer's behavior', *Economica*, New Series 5; 61–71.

––––– (1979) *Foundations of Economic Analysis*, New York: Atheneum, 1979.

Say, Jean-Baptiste (1845) *A Treatise on Political Economy*, 4th edn, trans. by C. R. Prinsep, Philadelphia: Grigg and Elliot.

––––– (1967) *A Catechism in Political Economy*, trans. by John Richter, New York: Augustus M. Kelley.

Schneider, Erich (1952) *Pricing and Equilibrium*, trans. by T. W. Hutchinson, New York: Macmillan.

––––– (1975) *Joseph A. Schumpeter*, trans. by W. E. Kuhn, Lincoln, Neb.: Bureau of Business Research.

Schultz, Henry (1927) 'Theoretical considerations relating to supply', *Journal of Political Economy* 35; 437–64.

––––– (1929) 'Marginal productivity and the general pricing process', *Journal of Political Economy* 37; 505–51.

––––– (1932) 'Marginal productivity and the Lausanne School', *Economica*, New Series 12; 285–96.

Schumpeter, Joseph A. (1928) 'The instability of capitalism', *Economic Journal* 38; 361–86.

––––– (1934) *The Theory of Economic Development*, Cambridge, Mass.: Harvard University Press.

––––– (1939) *Business Cycles*, New York: McGraw-Hill.

––––– (1942) *Capitalism, Socialism, and Democracy*, New York: Harper and Brothers Publishers.

––––– (1947) 'The creative response in economic history', *Journal of Economic History* 7; 149–59.

———— (1954) *History of Economic Analysis*, Elizabeth B. Schumpeter (ed.), New York: Oxford University Press.

Scitovsky, Tibor (1943) 'A note on profit maximisation and its implications', *Review of Economic Studies* 11; 57–60.

———— (1951) *Welfare and Competition*, Chicago: Richard D. Irwin.

Shackle, G. L. S. (1969) *Decision, Order, and Time in Human Affairs* 2nd edn, Cambridge: Cambridge University Press.

Shephard, Ronald W. (1953) *Cost and Production Functions*, Princeton: Princeton University Press.

Smith, Steven H. (1984) 'Schumpeter's vision of the economic process,' unpublished manuscript.

Smithies, Arthur (1936) 'The boundaries of the production function and the utility function', in A. Smithies (ed.) *Explorations in Economics*, New York: McGraw-Hill, 326–35.

Spengler, J. J. and Allen, W. R. (eds) (1960) *Essays in Economic Thought: Aristotle to Marshall*, Chicago: Rand McNally.

Sraffa, Pierro (1926) 'The laws of returns under competitive conditions', *Economic Journal* 36; 535–50.

Stark, W. (1952) *Jeremy Bentham's Economic Writings*, London: George Allen and Unwin Ltd.

Stigler, George J. (1941) *Production and Distribution Theories: 1870 to 1895*, New York: Macmillan and Co.

———— (1942) *The Theory of Competitive Price*, New York: The Macmillan Co.

———— (1965) *Essays in the History of Economics*, Chicago: University of Chicago Press.

Strauss, James H. (1944) 'The entrepreneur: The firm', *Journal of Political Economy* 52; 112–27.

Tarascio, Vincent J. (1974) 'Pareto on political economy', *History of Political Economy* 6; 361–80.

Tarascio, Vincent J. and Caldwell, Bruce (1979) 'Theory choice in economics: Philosophy and practice', *Journal of Economic Issues* 13; 983–1006.

von Thunen, Johann (1966) *The Isolated State*, trans. by Carla M. Wartenburg, Peter Hall (ed.), Oxford: Pergamon Press.

Tuttle, Charles A. (1927) 'Function of the entrepreneur', *American Economic Review* 17; 13–25.

———— (1927) 'The entrepreneur in economic literature', *Journal of Political Economy* 35; 501–21.

Veblen, Thorstein B. (1904) *The Theory of Business Enterprise*, New York: Charles Scribner's Sons.

Viner, Jacob (1958) *The Long View and the Short*, Glencoe, Ill.: The Free Press.

Walras, Leon (1954) *Elements of Pure Economics*, trans. by William Jaffe, Homewood, Ill.: Richard D. Irwin.

Watson, Donald S. (1963) *Price Theory and Its Uses*, Boston: Houghton Mifflin Co.

Weston, Fred J. (1954) 'The profit concept and theory: A restatement', *Journal of Political Economy* 62; 152–70.

Wicksell, Knut (1934–5) *Lectures on Political Economy*, trans. by E. Classen, L. Robbins (ed.), New York: Macmillan and Co.

Wicksteed, Philip (1894) *Essay on the Co-ordination of the Laws of Distribution*, London: Macmillan and Co.

—— (1933) *The Common Sense of Political Economy and Selected Papers and Reviews on Economic Theory*, London: Routledge and Kegan Paul, Ltd.

Wilken, Paul H. (1979) *Entrepreneurship: A Comparative and Historical Study*, Norwood, N. J.: ABLEX Publishing Corp.

Williams, Philip (1978) *The Emergence of the Theory of the Firm*, London: Macmillan Press.

Wiseman, Jack (1980) 'Costs and decisions', in David A. Currie and Will Peters (eds) *Contemporary Economic Analysis*, vol. 2, London: Croom Helm.

Wood, Adrian (1975) *A Theory of Profits*, Cambridge: Cambridge University Press.

Young, Allyn (1928) 'Increasing returns and economic progress', *Economic Journal* 38; 527–42.

Zassenhaus, Herbert (1935–6) 'Dr. Schneider and the Theory of Production', *Review of Economic Studies* 3; 35–9.

Zeuthen, F. (1955) *Economic Theory and Method*, Cambridge: Harvard University Press.

Index

Index

53–4, 58; a factor of production
65, 115; not a factor of
production 18, 36, 57; as owner
34, 36–8, 41–2, 62–3;
remuneration of 11–14, 19–21,
35, 38, 41; as speculator 34–6,
43; *see also* arbitrageur;
coordinator; decision-maker;
innovator; profits; risk-bearer;
uncertainty
entrepreneur, disappearance of
1–2, 140–1; as arbitrageur
113–14; as coordinator 110–12;
historical evidence 95–8; as
innovator 108–9; as uncertainty-
bearer 54, 109–10
entrepreneurship: consistency
over 132–5; demand for 11–12;
supply of 12, 14, 30, 61–2; a
threat to modern theory 132–3

factor immobility 113
factor market analysis 70, 72–4,
80, 87, 89–91, 105, 122, 125,
127
factor returns 31; factor shares 125
factors of production 9–10, 36,
62–3, 110, 115; traded and non-
traded 52–3 *see also* capital;
enterprise; entrepreneur;
labor; land; organization
Fetter, F. A. 59
firm, equilibrium 80–83;
optimization problem 105, 122,
127, 132
firm, theory of 54, 120;
consistency in 121–31, 141;
historical development 71–95;
postulates 102–7, 140–1
Fisher, I. 49, 55–6, 58, 78, 94
Friedman, M. 120, 142
Frisch, R. 93, 134–5

general equilibrium theory 15, 23,
50–1, 53, 71, 80–6, 113–14
Georgescu-Roegen, N. 93, 119,
133, 142

goods and services, classification
system 23–4

Harrod, R. F. 77–8, 93–4
Hawley, F. B. 34, 36–9, 41, 43,
49, 56, 58–9, 109, 139
Hayek, F. von 15
Herbert, R. F. 6
Hicks, J. R. 71, 80, 88–90, 92–4,
96
Higgs, H. 34
High, J. 15
Hotelling, H. 93, 124
human action 15–18, 20–1
human elements 143
human industry 7–8, 10–12; *see
also* labor; workman

income distribution *see*
distribution
indifference analysis 78–9, 86
information 10, 18–19; imperfect
143; perfect 102, 105–6, 109,
111–12, 114, 132
innovation 28, 42; no modern
theory of 108; types of 31, 60
innovator, entrepreneur as 4–5,
22–33, 49, 53–4, 59–62
inputs *see* factor market analysis
intuition 29
isoquant 70, 78–9, 83–4, 86–7,
89–90, 92, 104, 122

Jaffe, W. 83–4
Jevons, W. 48, 86
Johnson, W. E. 79, 86, 94

Kahn, R. F. 93
Kaldor, N. 65, 93
Kay, N. M. 112, 142
Kirzner, I. M. 5–6, 14–21, 33, 41,
43, 114, 139
Knight, F. H. 5 , 34, 43, 59, 64,
66, 93, 96, 98, 106, 109, 112,
139, 140
Koolman, G. 7

labor 7, 9, 39; directed 24, 27;

154

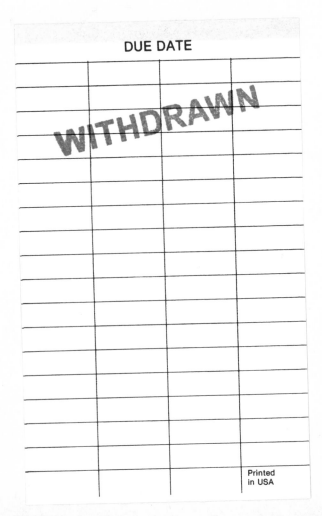

DUE DATE

WITHDRAWN

Printed
in USA